Do the
RIGHT
THING

Do the RIGHT THING

PR Tips for a Skeptical Public

JAMES HOGGAN

with Richard Littlemore

Capital Ideas for Business

CAPITAL
BOOKS, INC.
Sterling, Virginia

Capital Books, Inc.
P.O. Box 605
Herndon, Virginia 20172-0605

ISBN 13: 978-1-933102-86-3

Library of Congress Cataloging-in-Publication Data
Hoggan, James.
Do the right thing : PR tips for a skeptical public / James Hoggan with Richard D. Littlemore.
p. cm.
ISBN 978-1-933102-85-6 (alk. paper)
1. Public relations. I. Littlemore, Richard D. II. Title.

HD59.H595 2009
659.2—dc22

2009010923

Printed in the United States of America on acid-free paper that meets the American National Standards Institute Z39-48 Standard.

First Edition

10 9 8 7 6 5 4 3 2 1

*To my wife Enid Marion who has been
working on my communication skills
since we were kids.*

*And to my friend John Lefebvre who
has taught me the importance of
pure intention.*

More Praise for *Do the Right Thing*

"Jim Hoggan and Richard Littlemore have written the Thinking Person's Guide to Public Relations. It needed to be done. Too many flack books ignore the research base of communications practice, as well as the obligation that those who mess with public opinion have to the rest of us. Steeped in practice but tempered by values, this book situates each case in a conceptual challenge. It is both pragmatic and intellectual. If you want to know both how to do public relations and why to do it, this is a great book."

—SUSAN NALL BALES, PRESIDENT, FRAMEWORKS INSTITUTE, WASHINGTON, D.C.

"This is a must read for one who wishes to effectively connect and communicate with others. Jim has provided a simple and succinct roadmap to master the art of communication."

—THOMAS SKIDMORE, PRESIDENT & CEO, GLENTEL INC.

Contents

Foreword

Among journalists, there is one phrase that sums up their feelings about the public relations industry: "the dark side." When reporters or editors leave the news media for employment in PR, this is where they are seen to go—from light into darkness.

On first blush, it makes sense. Journalists believe that while they are out to expose the truth, the public relations industry is bent on managing the message. But if you examine what journalists actually do, you might be surprised at how much they rely on having good relationships with public relations professionals. Journalists look to their PR contacts for accurate and timely information, and for a clear line to the right authority figure. Public relations representatives, meanwhile, need to preserve their own integrity and that of the organizations they represent.

It was 2002 when Jim Hoggan and I first started talking about the newspaper contribution that led to this book. I had recently been appointed business editor at *The Vancouver Sun* and I was seeking ways to engage with readers. When I heard that Jim was looking to share his career experience with a wide audience, we got together over lunch and tossed around a few ideas. Initially, we talked about him penning longer articles; but I wanted something shorter, a contrast to our usual offering. Over lunch at Aqua Riva restaurant, overlooking the cruise ship terminal where tourists embark for Alaska, we worked out the plan: once-a-week tips, no more than 100 words each.

Those tips ran in *The Vancouver Sun* for five years. I liked that they flew in the face of convention by exposing the basic truth that *how* one communicates is as consequential as *what* one communicates. I also liked that they were honest and forthright. Implicitly and often explicitly, Jim made it clear that retaining integrity was not simply about mouthing the right words; it was about doing the right thing and then telling a story clearly. I believe he related his experience honestly and for the right reasons; and that is why, collected together in book form, the tips make for such interesting reading.

There is always going to be a dividing line between journalism and public relations. Let's not be naïve. But I respect the way Jim shone a light on that relationship. Journalists who followed the Tips series stood to learn as much as our regular readers.

More than anything else, what sold me on Jim Hoggan's PR Tips was that he showed so much courage and vision in his many non-profit activities, including his work with environmentalist David Suzuki and his mission to hold the petroleum industry to account on global-warming issues. This underscored for me that while his firm had many powerful clients with all kinds of motivations for seeking to manage their message, Jim really did have a genuine interest in making the world a better place through better communications.

STEWART MUIR
BUSINESS MANAGER
CANWEST NEWS SERVICES

Preface

This is a book about public relations. It's a book about relationships and reputation, about communication and trust. It's a book about public and private conversation—about making yourself understood in a noisy and confusing world.

That makes it a book for everyone. Few of us can afford the complications (or expense) that can arise from being *mis*understood. All of us can benefit by being more persuasive. All of us rely on our credibility—to be convincing and, sometimes, just to be believed. And whether it is a personal reputation or a corporate brand, a good public image can have incalculable value.

As you pick through the pages to come, you will find two distinct sections. First up, you'll find "Strategy: The Basics, the Background, and the Big Ideas." This is intended as a kind of PR primer, beginning with our definition of public relations and our overarching philosophy on how to practice the art in a way that will reap the greatest benefit for your clients, for you, and for society as a whole. Then, we delve into some of the forces that affect everyone working in the communications industry—some of the dark forces of the past and some of the dazzling changes brought on by the Internet and by all of modern communications technology. We talk about things every good communicator should understand: the history of storytelling, the importance of framing, the art of dialogue, and the secrets of persuasion. Finally, we share a crisis management case study that pulls a lot of this theory into one practical example.

The second section we call "Tactics: Hands-On Tips for Everyday Success," and this is really where the book got started. For more than three years, the whole team at Hoggan & Associates worked on these tips, preparing them one-by-one for a weekly series that we produced for our local newspaper, *The Vancouver Sun*. We started, at the invitation of then-business editor Stewart Muir, with some PR fundamentals—how to organize a news conference or prepare for a presentation—but the longer we worked, the more deeply we drilled into our own experience and understanding. Each week we would get together, choose a topic, and then thrash out what we felt was the central lesson. Then, we charged our favorite writer, Richard Littlemore, with the task of whittling this "collected wisdom" down to 100 words or less—and we circulated that draft for edits and comments until we were sure we had the point right. It was a rigorous exercise in figuring out what is most critical and then saying it succinctly.

We hope now that you will be able to make use of that effort. It is intended that you should be able to pick up this book in a moment of doubt, a moment of crisis, or a moment of discovery and flip to the section that speaks to that momentary concern.

In some cases, you might find a single piece of advice that answers your question. In others, you might find a series of tips or a whole chapter that expands your understanding. In every case, you will find evidence of knowledge accumulated over many careers.

In that regard, I want to make it clear that while my name is on the cover, a large team has contributed to the content of this book. I must credit all of my colleagues at Hoggan & Associates, past and present, who participated in this process. I also want to thank 30 years worth of clients—business and public sector leaders who taught me as many lessons as I could ever hope to teach them. And I must acknowledge input from other professionals, from the researchers, designers, planners, lawyers, and consultants to whom I have gone for advice over the decades—and whom I will call again whenever I can. Finally, special thanks is due Stewart Muir, now business manager for *Canwest News Services*. Without Stewart's interest and the newspaper's discipline, I might never have assembled this information in such a highly usable form.

Now, please, read on. Whether you start with the user's guide or leap straight to the tips, read what you need. Pick little bits or whole chapters. Grab the advice you want right now, or dig down for the insight that will make all of your communications efforts more effective. However you approach it, I hope you enjoy the book as much as we have enjoyed putting it together, and I hope that the wisdom collected here serves you as well as it has served us.

—JIM HOGGAN

Acknowledgments

The names on the cover of this book do insufficient justice to the creative crowd of people who contribute to its contents. The most senior team members (present and past) at Hoggan & Associates were critical putting all this together—especially Kristin Treat who got the book published and forced us to make our deadline and Nancy McHarg for sharing her cautious second thoughts, Nancy Spooner, Karen Cook, Terry McDonald, and Chris Freimond who helped think through many of the early tips. Terry contributed extensively to the investor relations section. DeSmogBlog manager Kevin Grandia was invaluable on the subject of social media. And Erin Gawne carried the administrative burden with cheerful persistence. Maria Lescerbo who setup the lunch that started us on the path to publishing this book.

The We also enjoyed a huge amount of help from outside experts, many of them named in the pages of the book. Frequent Hoggan consultant Terry Castle offered brilliant insights in the public speaking section. Former QLT Inc. CFO Ken Galbraith gave us fabulous material in the mergers and acquisitions section and former Vancouver city planner Larry Beasley shared his wisdom on public consultation. Urban Development Institute executive director Maureen Enser and former Catalyst Paper vice president Stu Clugtson offered feedback and ideas based on their years of experience. My long-time friend Mike Sullivan was also generous and patient with advice and mentoring that was always invaluable.

Another group of contributors, similarly invaluable, includes the fine researchers whose work we have come to rely on in recent years. These include Susan Nall Bales of the Frameworks Institute, Angus McAllister of McAllister Opinion Research, Evi Mustel of the Mustel Group, Steve Rosell of Viewpoint Learning, and Ed Wachtman of StoryTellings.

I would like to acknowledge and thank all these people for their contributions to this book and for all that they have done for Hoggan & Associates and for me personally. Public relations is a necessarily collaborative business and any success associated with my name must also be credited to these and to all the people I have worked with through the years.

Finally, I would like to acknowledge my closest collaborator in this project, Richard Littlemore. Richard has long had a knack for writing down the things that I say in the way I wish I had said them. He also has been tireless in rewriting, editing, and rewriting again as my thinking has progressed and as others have offered input and advice. The evidence of his skill rests on every page and I can personally attest to his patience and good humor. Doing the *Write* Thing together has been a great pleasure.

This book is the work of a lifetime, something I am proud to have done and, again, that I could never have done alone. I want to say thank you—Thank You!—to all of those who made it possible.

PART ONE

Strategy: The Basics, the Background,
and the Big Ideas

1

Finding the Right Thing to Do: A User's Guide to Public Relations Success

In every new venture, in every crisis—in every brush with fame or ignominy—there are always those moments when you think: What should I do now? How can I manage this situation or mend that reputation? What's the best way to raise my profile or attract media attention? What, in today's circumstance, is the right thing to do?

In lots of little and specific ways, this book proposes to answer that question. The following pages are filled with tactics and techniques that have proven to be "right" for us and for many others.

But the practice of public relations is much more than the sum of these parts, because getting—and keeping—a good reputation is not purely a question of tactics. No matter how clever your communications team, you cannot *create* credibility or *instill* confidence. Reputations are not built on press releases and glossy brochures. They are built on performance. If, in this age of cynicism, you want employee loyalty, consumer trust, and a degree of public regard, you have to earn it. And once you have it, you cannot neglect it.

You also want the reputation you deserve—no more and certainly no less. This is a matter of balance. A good and widespread reputation will serve the goals of most businesses and individuals. But you don't want your reputation to get ahead of reality. Sudden and widespread acclaim can be great for stock promoters whose goal is to make a quick buck and move on to the next play. But undeserved fame can be a long-term disaster for a company that can't meet inflated expectations. Many individuals have felt the devastating sting of a disappointed public. Many corporations with perfectly sustainable business models have watched their profits tank when the market concluded that corporate promises couldn't be believed.

So, before you jump to the tips—the public relations tactics that we employ day to day—it might help to know something about the Hoggan approach, something about our overarching public relations strategy. Over 30 years, we have developed a unique prism through which we look at everything we do. It's a test, comprised of three guiding rules.

1. Do the right thing.
2. Be seen to be doing the right thing.
3. Don't get #1 and #2 mixed up.

This is simple and complicated at the same time. Doing the right thing is fundamental; and in a small town, it might actually be enough. No one needs communications advice when everyone is already well acquainted, just as no one can rescue the reputation of a small town grocer who overcharges or a barber who can't cut hair.

But in our world—in a populous, complex, media-dominated society—you can't sit around and assume that everyone will notice that you have done something right, or stopped doing something wrong. You must take your reputation in your own hands. You must make sure that people see when you are doing the right thing.

That said, you'll find nothing but grief if you get caught pandering— if you pretend to do the right thing or if the public begins to believe you are making positive changes only because you have been forced to do so. All the world may be a stage, but if people think you're play-acting, you're apt to discover how quickly and easily a good reputation can be lost.

At some point, finding the right thing to do is a value judgment. If you can keep that in mind, this book will help you do the rest.

What Is Public Relations, Anyway?

This is a question that might seem obvious to most business people—particularly to those of you who have hired public relations consultants in the past. Depending on your experience, you might think that public relations is what you do when you are trying to get out of trouble or into the news. Many businesspeople who are generally confident in their own abilities still call for help in a crisis. Many acknowledge the value that public relations people can bring in getting public attention: everything from creating and distributing press releases and kits to media training and media relations. Businesses are also inclined to turn to PR agencies for things like speech writing or event coordination, for investor relations, or reputation management. And sophisticated businesses will have had experience with public relations preoccupations like "key messages" and "positioning," taking advantage of skills in what we think of as storytelling.

But that touches on some of what public relations people do, without answering why they do it. It canvases tactics without getting to the central question: What *is* public relations?

Here's one answer: Public relations is the art and science of earning credibility and building goodwill among all those who are important to your business.

Public relations is not advertising and it's *not* spin. It is not the practice of backslapping guys with big-checked sport coats and damp hands—people who would peddle their influence with malleable members of the media or use questionable tactics to manipulate public opinion over the short term. On the contrary, those are the people who have done the most damage in the past to the reputation of the public relations industry itself and to the reputations of the companies and institutions that they once served.

They were sometimes successful in making a name for their companies, but they too often found that fame was a double-edged sword. Good public relations is about ensuring that as you develop your reputation, you do so for the right reasons. And if you already have a high public profile, it's about managing your reputation, through good times and bad.

If achieving credibility and goodwill are the goals, then mutual understanding is a fundamental building block. You have to start with a clear grasp of your own ambitions—and your role in the community. You must understand how your goals and the community's values overlap (or conflict), and you must have a sense of what people in the community expect—what they have a right to expect—from you. By working this out—by discovering exactly where the public interest intersects with your own goals—you can set the best direction for your business and design a communication strategy that will win the greatest amount of public support.

In this process, you cannot hope to communicate *at* your audience. All good conversations run two ways. You must be able to articulate your own position in a clear and engaging way. But most people won't listen long to someone who isn't listening back. So, in addition to making your own case well, you must listen. You must pay attention to your audience's position, and you must monitor whether and to what degree they are hearing and understanding what you are trying to say. Finally, you must be willing to allow the conversation—and perhaps your position—to change in the process. Only by being responsive will you show your good faith.

This is particularly important in the current climate of mistrust. People are not just tired of cute advertising and glib public relations spin—they are openly hostile to it. They have grown disillusioned and distrustful—and if people don't trust you, it is very difficult for them to hear what you are saying.

The Internet has also made communications more challenging. You can no longer hunker down in a crisis and plan an unhurried response.

If you hesitate in this age of hyper-awareness, the bloggers will define the story before you even begin. It has always been the case that the first person who gets out with new information "frames" the story, creating in the minds of the audience an impression that is difficult to update or contradict. Today, more than ever in history, you have to react fast to be first.

You also have to establish your credibility, something that is done best when you are *not* reacting to events. Given public cynicism, you must start by being transparent. That doesn't mean laying bare trade secrets. It means building a reputation for honesty—for speaking the truth when it serves you, and especially, acknowledging the truth when it hurts.

You can't do this one time and think it will be enough. Stakeholders, shareholders, clients, and customers—audience members of whatever kind—will give you their trust in measured doses. You can't buy credibility or invent it overnight. You have to earn it. You have to establish your reputation carefully and over time.

Then, if people feel they know you—if they understand your goals and priorities—they won't be surprised when you try to defend your interests. They may even be sympathetic. If people trust you, if they find that you are clear and forthright in your positions, they are more likely to find your arguments persuasive. They will give you the benefit of the doubt.

The wrinkle in all of this is that communicating with a broad public audience is infinitely more complex than, say, gathering your executive team together for a planning session or a briefing. Communications can be tricky enough in your personal and private relationships. We all know the joys and frustrations of trying to make ourselves understood to our spouses, our parents, or our children.

But the rules change when you start dealing, at Internet speeds, with crowds—with people who don't know you and have no reason to trust what you say. The most complicating factor of all is the participation— the sometimes infuriating but often essential participation—of the media. No matter how good you think you are as a communicator, if you have relationships with the media, you need to put some specific energy into building this unique and necessary skill set.

There are many facets to good public relations—communications and research, crisis planning and management, media relations and public speaking. Some are more complicated than others and some are more critical in certain circumstances. But none is a frill.

The civilized world exists largely on goodwill. We communicate, we collaborate, we cooperate. We build small businesses, huge industries, and great halls for entertainment and governance. We do so in our own interest and in the "public interest."

Ultimately, public relations is the process of aligning those interests for everyone's benefit. And if that's what you're trying to do, this is the best way to do it.

Ethical Public Relations: The Golden Rules

There is an old story, perhaps apocryphal, about a wealthy New York businessman who hires a senior public relations consultant. The businessman calls the consultant into the first meeting and says, "I have a reputation for being a real S.O.B. and I want you to change that."

The PR consultant responds: "Absolutely. But first you'll have to stop being an S.O.B."

The moral is this: You don't come by your reputation accidentally. For good or ill, you earn it. Whether as a single individual or a large organization, odds are that sooner or later you will wind up with the reputation you deserve.

But, just because you don't get a reputation accidentally, doesn't mean that you might not acquire one inadvertently or—sometimes worse—that you may never establish a reputation at all.

If you care about your public image—and if you are not satisfied to have that image defined by critics and competitors—you must come back to our three steps.

1. Do the Right Thing

This is not just a moral injunctive. Doing the right thing may speak to your values and your integrity. But it is also a strategy for success.

I came to this conclusion early in my career. At least, I noticed early how dangerous it was to think you could do something less than the right thing and still maintain a good reputation. Specifically, I noticed that every time someone tried to delay or dilute the release of bad news, things tended to go straight downhill. The media grew restless and hostile; and when the information finally came out (as it usually did), the crisis got worse.

I also noticed that when people did the right thing—when they stepped up quickly, acknowledging a problem, posing a solution, and setting out a plan to make sure a crisis wouldn't recur—things almost invariably got better. I found, again and again, that the public is remarkably receptive to a sincere apology; that people will forgive almost anything but deceit. I found that doing the right thing was a business strategy that works.

It works in a crisis, and it works the rest of the time, too. A good reputation comes from doing the right thing all the time.

Mind you, recognizing "the right thing" is part of the challenge. We all can tell the difference between the unadorned truth and a carefully conceived lie, even if the latter can seem like a tempting way to put off trouble. But sometimes what's right is a matter of perspective. Something that looks right from an efficiency standpoint might not be right when it comes to safety. What's right for a short-term investor— what you think is right for the bottom line today—might not serve the company's reputation over time, creating a situation in which you reap an economic gain in the short term only to surrender even more value down the road.

Our agency periodically gets called in by companies that want our help introducing a particular proposal to the public. Often, the company has decided on a plan without consulting very widely and has suddenly found itself with a "public relations problem." We generally respond in these circumstances with a round of research—formal or informal—and often we find a sharp difference of opinion as to what might be considered the right thing to do.

At such times—and in times of crisis—"doing the right thing" can be a real test of character. For example, Hoggan & Associates won a Silver Anvil Award (one of the PR industry's highest honors) for our work with an organic food store called Capers, now a subsidiary of Whole Foods. Capers discovered that an employee who had served in food preparation was suffering from Hepatitis A—a worrisome piece of information that community health officials shared immediately with the public. Management's first response was to shut down the food preparation area for all of Capers' deli counters—a decision that was not at all "right" for their short-term business, but one that quickly impressed customers with Capers' determination to put safety ahead of profit. The Capers brand is stronger today than ever. (For a more complete description, see chapter 7.)

There is another side to this argument, a side that speaks directly to the cynicism of today's most opportunistic companies. The great American critic and journalist H.L. Mencken once said that, "No one in this world has ever lost money by underestimating the intelligence of the great masses of the plain people." And the tobacco peddlers at Philip Morris and the swindlers at Enron have taken advantage of that fact. They did what was right for them, regardless of whether it was—in any responsible way—the right thing to do. They made a specialty out of a certain, highly questionable kind of public relations and they proved that deceit can work—for a while. But I believe that good guys win in the end.

I also believe that Mencken may have been wrong about the intelligence of crowds. People sometimes do foolish things, but you're courting disaster if you treat them like fools.

Malcolm Gladwell, the talented staff writer for the *New Yorker* magazine, offered one explanation in his bestseller, *Blink*. In his introduction, Gladwell said that his book is about "rapid cognition, about the kind of thinking that happens in a blink of an eye." He said, "When you meet someone for the first time, or walk into a house you are thinking of buying, or read the first few sentences of a book, your mind takes about two seconds to jump to a series of conclusions."

Gladwell argues that these conclusions, which seem intuitive rather than rational, are often remarkably accurate. That's because what seems like intuition is often something more: It is a reaction that is informed by a lifetime of experience, a lifetime of reading faces and assessing the credibility of information. I think there might be something else besides, because in my experience, people have an uncanny ability to sense a fraud. In a climate of mistrust, people have learned to recognize authenticity.

Again, spin might work for a while. Like a magician, you can sometimes catch the crowd looking the other way—for a while. But if your business plan doesn't involve a hasty, late-night departure from town, there is no substitute for doing the right thing.

2. Be Seen to Be Doing the Right Thing

We live in a complicated world—a world in which everyone seems to be competing for attention, a world in which every individual is overwhelmed by messages and images. In such a world, you cannot leave your reputation to chance. You cannot stand by while people with competing interests define your issue—or your company. You cannot hope that your clients, customers, or stakeholders will understand your position if you have not presented it forcefully, expertly, and in the right context and venues.

As for the media, it would be quaint but naïve to believe that they are there only to pass on objective information. Reporters bring their own perspective—and the pressures of their own highly competitive business. They must sell a product and the appeal of that product often depends on things like conflict. There is no reason to think ill of the media, to fear or resent reporters and editors. But you have to remember that they have their own agenda, and it doesn't necessarily include the careful dissemination of *your* message.

In such an environment—in communicating with a disillusioned and skeptical public—you can't just do the right thing and hope that someone will notice. Actions may speak louder than words, but in the crowded media conversation of today, your actions can be overlooked or badly misunderstood.

This becomes tricky on two counts. First, no one likes a braggart, and second, unless you have already built a reputation for integrity, any effort to tout your own strengths may actually attract negative attention. But remember, this is not about being boastful or being a media hound. It's a matter of making sure that the people who are important to your business know what you are doing.

Sometimes, you will need help—testimonials from credible people who are willing to speak up on your behalf. But remember this too: In order to win that validation—in order to attract reputable leaders who are willing to confirm your credibility—you need to be doing the right thing. Which leads to the third point.

3. Don't Get #1 and #2 Mixed Up

This is the tricky bit. If you do the right thing *because* it's the right thing to do, people will respect you for it. But if you forget yourself in a flurry of PR tactics and strategies—if you start thinking primarily about the public relations implications of your actions, and only secondarily about what's right—things can easily go wrong.

In other words, people want to see you doing the right thing; they *don't* want to see you doing PR. So, keep #1 and #2 in order. Do the right thing for its own sake—and *then* think about the best way to make sure that the people who are important to your business hear about it.

A Strategy for Every Day

We come once again to the suggestion that public relations is inevitably tied up with decisions about values—about right and wrong.

That is not necessarily the case. There are lots of occasions—probably a huge majority—in which your tactical decisions have nothing to do with a value judgment about what is right or wrong. For example, writing a speech, preparing a brochure, giving media training or presentation tips to the CEO, organizing a news conference, there are hundreds of things you can do that are just good effective tactics in the search for fair play in the media and for understanding from your stakeholder groups.

It's also true that even though you try, every day, to do what is right, things will still go wrong. People will make mistakes, machinery will break down. Communications challenges—and opportunities—will come and go. You won't be facing a gut-wrenching decision about right and wrong—you'll just be staring into a crowd of reporters, or shareholders, who all want to hear the news.

Sometimes, too, there is no obvious right answer that will bring everyone back to your side. Sometimes there are legitimate differences of opinion as to what's right and wrong. Sometimes there are irreconcilable differences among people of good faith. Nobody said business was going to be easy.

But that still leaves a risk for everyone who is engaged in the practice of public relations. When the going gets tough, it's hard to avoid obsessing about the tactics and strategies of reputation management— and forgetting about the big picture. It's tempting to flip to the appropriate page and seek out the tip that will put your company in the best possible light, regardless of whether it involves actually doing the *right* thing.

When you get to that moment—of obsession or desperation—stop, if only for a moment, and think about the three rules. Ask yourself whether the decision you are about to make would attract the support of your reasonable critics—whether *they* will think that it was the right thing to do. If the answer is yes, you will have a strong foundation on which to build a good reputation.

▼

That brings us back, finally and again, to the fundamental question: What is public relations? For us, it is the art of figuring out the right thing to do and—in the most complex communications environment the world has ever known—letting people know that we are doing it.

We have already made the point that spin doesn't work in a small town—that poor performance can't prevail when people are keeping track. Well, our world—vast, crowded, and confusing though it may be—is becoming more and more like a small town. The breadth, scope, and speed of communications are removing the protection of distance. The age of secrets is coming to an end.

The world is also becoming less physically forgiving. There are no longer any new seas to discover or new forests to plunder. There is only one huge and increasingly crowded planet whose finite resources we overspend at our peril.

In this age of awareness and accountability, the golden rules of public relations will do more than save your reputation; they may well save us all.

So:

1. Do the right thing.
2. Be seen to be doing the right thing; and
3. Don't get #1 and #2 mixed up.

If you take nothing else away from this book, take that. Your clients, customers, shareholders, stakeholders, partners, employees— their children and their children's children—will all thank you for it.

2

Darth Vader PR:
The Lure of the Dark Side

About 20 years ago I was sitting in the boardroom of a Vancouver technology company, brainstorming with the senior executive team about how to deal with a bit of bad news—a developmental disappointment. This was a hot property, already a market darling, and anything we said was sure to catch the analysts' attention. In such circumstances, managers are always worried about the consequences of spooking the investment community. In some cases, a large sale by a single large investor can be catastrophic for a high-tech firm in this start-up phase.

The problem is that this particular company had already been "protecting shareholder value" a little too aggressively. There had been a string of setbacks and each had been announced to the market in a way that now might be characterized as overly optimistic. The company had not lied. But as its understatements piled up, one on the other, the actual conditions of its current operation were moving further away from market perception—and further away from reality. As a result, we faced the challenge of dribbling out another unhappy press release and doing so in a way that didn't endanger the company—but also didn't compound the growing disconnect between hard facts and an overly rosy market impression. The more we struggled, the further we seemed from a solution.

Then, in one of those tired silences that pass for a period of reflection, I asked what turned out to be a fortuitous question. I asked, "What would be the *right* thing to do?"

A riffle of discomfort seemed to pass through the room. These were good people—honest and responsible—who had been working sincerely, and extremely hard, to make the company a success. There was no doubt in my mind that each of them had every intention of doing the right thing. But, up to this moment, that had not been the question that we had been trying to answer. This was a public relations brainstorm and we had found ourselves thinking exclusively about public relations tactics. We had lost sight of the real issue—of what I now believe is the most important consideration in every public relations conversation.

It's interesting that when we turned the question around—when we asked, "What IS the right thing to do?"—the problem became easier. We didn't come instantly to a solution, but we could see our direction more clearly. As it turned out, we wrote the disappointing press release and then followed up with a more formal and thorough market "update," in which the CEO traveled to major markets and laid out every bit of bad news—in cold, clear, and unvarnished detail. Perversely, the stock price went up. The company won accolades for being forthright. It seemed that almost everyone else was as "heavily invested" in the firm as we were.

It seemed that doing the right thing was the right thing to do.

If I had ever had doubts before, this incident cleared them up. The more I thought about it afterwards, the more I realized two things. First, the truth will usually catch up to you in the end. Any PR campaign that is less than forthright is heading at high speed for a rocky shoal. The only surprise will be when the impact actually occurs.

Second, this is not a question that can be left to chance: If you stop asking yourself, "What's the right thing to do?" the risk of getting caught in the spin trap is all but unavoidable. Think about this very situation, a version of which arises all the time. Whenever any client has bad news to announce, we always ask, for the record, "Are you looking for a news release that is honest and direct?" And people always say, "Absolutely." Then we put the cold truth on paper and say, "Do you want a news release that says this?" And, almost inevitably, they say, "No!"

The truth hurts. At least, it can seem painful in the short term.

In the avoidance of this pain, however, the public relations industry has seen some very dark days. In ignoring that fundamental question, some very clever PR practitioners have explored the far reaches of public deception and manipulation. And some have enjoyed outrageous personal success in the process. But as I survey the scene today, I can see too clearly the damage that has been done to public trust and to the reputation of my chosen profession.

This came most unavoidably to my attention in 2007 through a big piece of Canadian research. The pollster Angus Reid had asked Canadians who they found to be credible on issues relating to the environment. Some of the answers were, perhaps, obvious: 77 percent of respondents said they believe what they hear from scientists; and 62 percent said they believe environmental organizations. But some of the other ratings were terrible: Only 23 percent of the people said they believe environmental news they hear from the federal government. Just 11 percent said they believe industry and only 9 percent said they accept what they hear from industry associations.

Government, industry, and industry associations—in the communications business, those are our clients and they appeared to have lost the public trust. This realization led me to launch a new piece of research, asking the painful question: If the public doesn't think highly of our clients, what do they think of public relations? Actually, we asked a two-part question, first in Canada and later in the U.S., as well. We asked: "Which of the following statements best represents your own opinion of the role and function performed by public relations experts?"

The choices were:

1. PR experts help the public better understand the environmental performance of companies by providing clear and accurate information, or
2. PR experts help deceive the public by making the environmental performance of companies appear better than it really is.

Here's the quite horrifying result: In North America, 81 percent of respondents said they thought we were helping our clients misrepresent their performance. That means, when it comes to the environment, four out of five people think that we mislead people for a living.

Given some of the dark history of PR, you can hardly blame them. The record is littered with stories of spin and manipulation.

One of the greatest of such stories was written by Edward Bernays (1891-1995), often referred to as "the father of public relations." Bernays, an Austrian immigrant to the U.S. and Sigmund Freud's nephew, is the person who coined the term "engineering consent." In his 1928 book *Propaganda,* he wrote:

> If we understand the mechanism and motives of the group mind, is it not possible to control and regiment the masses according to our will without their knowing about it? The recent practice of propaganda has proved that it is possible, at least up to a certain point and within certain limits.

Bernays' work was hailed widely at the time, and it continues to be taught in public relations courses today. It also would be foolish to take issue with some of what he says. Humans are not coldly rational in their decision-making. They are generally busy, a little harried, and appropriately obsessed with their own affairs. In most cases, it's hard to get their attention at all; and when you do, people often respond emotionally or on the basis of biases that may be a complete mystery to an advertiser, an advocate, or a politician hoping to engage in a straight conversation. Effective public relations requires a degree of subtlety and sometimes benefits from what might appear to be indirection.

But in using this kind of expertise on behalf of a client, PR people are directly affecting the public conversation. We risk taking advantage of free speech—confusing public thinking—and in the process we are undermining democracy. That should be a sobering reality for everyone—and it should attach a heavy weight of personal and public responsibility on every PR person and on everyone who is taking their advice.

Bernays actually recognized this—or paid lip service to it. He said that a public relations counsel (a term he appears to have coined), "must never accept a retainer or assume a position which puts his duty to the groups he represents above his duty to society."

Bernays then built a great career, faithfully exercising his duty to his clients in a way that often seemed to disadvantage society as a whole. Some of this was relatively harmless. For example, he organized the first known political pancake breakfast (for Calvin Coolidge). Given how little was known at the time about the dangers of smoking, you might also forgive him for organizing the Torches of Liberty parade in Manhattan in 1929. In one of the great "earned media" events of all time, he assembled a crowd of young women who took to the streets smoking Lucky Strikes. Bernays sold it as a march for women's rights, but the American Tobacco Company paid the bill—and got the benefit when women felt "liberated" enough to start smoking in public.

Less forgivable was his participation in the campaign (and ultimate CIA coup) to oust the democratically elected government of Guatemala in 1954, an incident that apparently put the interests of the United Fruit Company (now Chiquita Brands International) ahead of all others. Bernays also recorded, in his own autobiography, the information that Nazi propagandist Joseph Goebbels identified another of Bernays' early texts, *Crystallizing Public Opinion,* as having been a helpful resource in organizing the campaign against German Jews.

▼

For examples of "good tactics" in a bad cause, you can hardly do better than follow the history of big tobacco. Cigarette companies started small, giving cigarettes to soldiers and paying movie stars to smoke on screen, but the parades and publicity stunts became more reprehensible as our knowledge of the dangers of smoking increased. Philip Morris, for example, really crossed the line in the early 1990s with a PR campaign conceived by the PR firm APCO-Worldwide. Those were hard times for tobacco. Americans were quitting in large numbers and American governments were starting to restrict smoking in public places because of the dangers of second-hand smoke.

For years, Philip Morris had retained "scientific experts" who would vouch for the safety of smoking—or at least would swear that the dangers couldn't be proved unequivocally. But the public had wised up and the company knew that it needed a new routine.

APCO came to the rescue, suggesting that the public *might* believe a group of "independent" scientists. So, in 1993, the company proposed the formation of "a grassroots organization" called The Advancement of Sound Science Coalition, TASSC.

We know this today because APCO's original memos were made public in tobacco lawsuits during the 1990s. (Google "tobacco papers" for an exhaustive read.) In the memo proposing the formation of TASSC, APCO set out a media strategy that began with these objectives:

- Establish TASSC as a credible source for reporters when questioning the validity of scientific studies.
- Encourage the public to question—from the grassroots up—the validity of scientific studies.
- Mobilize support for TASSC through alliances with other organizations and third-party allies.
- Develop materials, including new article reprints, that can be "merchandized" to TASSC audiences.

The giveaway phrase in this paper is "from the grassroots up." Nothing in this campaign was ever assumed to have burbled up from an engaged public. All this "independent thought" was to be bought and paid for by Philip Morris. But APCO realized how obvious this would look if the tobacco giant was TASSC's only financial supporter. (The next strategy on this list was actually: "Increase membership in and funding of TASSC.") So APCO sent out recruitment letters to 20,000 businesses inviting them to join a fight for "sound science."

Through this gesture, and through years of related campaigning, Philip Morris, APCO, and TASSC reframed several legitimate public health questions as debatable issues of "junk science" and free choice. And again, if you think this was inadvertent, another APCO memo spells it out.

When APCO took TASSC to Europe, the company created a list to "Link the tobacco issue with . . . more 'politically correct' products." This they proposed as a potential list of regulatory issues that corporations could denounce as having been based on "junk science."

- Global warming
- Nuclear waste disposal
- Diseases and pests in agricultural products for trans border trade
- Biotechnology
- Eco labeling for EC products
- Food processing and packaging

TASSC, as it turns out, died with the tobacco lawsuits, its credibility in tatters. But many of its tactics—and several of the tacticians—are still in play. Most prominent among the tacticians is Steve Milloy, currently the proprietor of a website called JunkScience.com, and a columnist for Fox News since 2003. Milloy was still taking money from tobacco (and from Exxon Mobil) as late as 2005, information that Fox has never shared with its audience. Yet he continues to defend smoking, to question the science of global warming, to promote nuclear energy, and to condemn organic foods (in deference, perhaps, to his longstanding relationship as a registered lobbyist for the Monsanto corporation).

Another APCO alumnus is a Canadian named Tom Harris, now the head of a new "grassroots" organization called the International Climate Science Coalition (ICSC). At a 2008 meeting of activists and organizations still campaigning to spread doubt about the science of climate change, Harris gave a presentation that included this list of proposed tactics:

> We need regular high-impact media coverage of the findings of leading scientists—not just one or two publications, but we need to have hundreds all over the world. We need to have a high degree of information sharing and cooperation between groups, so that when (New Zealand's most prominent climate science critic) Vincent Gray for example has an article published in New Zealand, we can take the same piece and we can (say) submit it to newspapers all over North America and Europe.
>
> Then we have a nicely well-coordinated response, where letters to the editor and phone calls are made. "Congratulations on publishing that article!" You know, it's interesting because I've had many of my articles opposed so strongly, by environmentalists through phone calls and letters to the editor, that they just simply dry up, they just won't publish this again. So this does have feedback, I mean, these are people that run these newspapers, and they're scared, and impressed, and encouraged, depending on the feedback they get.
>
> We have to have grassroots organizations doing exactly that kind of thing: coordinated local activism.

"*Coordinated* local activism" is, of course, different from activism that is truly local. TASSC and the ICSC are nothing more than "Astro Turf groups"—fake grassroots organizations. (It's an interesting coincidence that the real Astro Turf is a Monsanto product.)

These examples are extreme, but many otherwise reasonable communications people get caught up using some version of these techniques. It begins the way we had begun in the resource company boardroom—by thinking of an important social or environmental issue as a "public relations problems." Soon, you start crafting ways to finesse the public issue rather than address the problem. And your critics, no matter how legitimate their concern, begin to look like adversaries rather than stakeholders (or sometimes victims). You reach into the APCO playbook and you come up with techniques like *astro-turfing*, *ventriloquism*, *truthiness* and *echo chamber*.

We've already talked about *astro-turfing*, and *ventriloquism* is obvious: You pay an "independent scientist" like the tobacco industry apologist Dr. S. Fred Singer to say something that wouldn't be credible if you said it yourself. (Singer is another TASSC alumnus who, like Milloy, has found a new life taking money from companies like Exxon Mobil and, coincidentally, putting himself forward as an expert in the argument against the science of climate change. His Science and Environmental Policy Project (SEPP) website, like Milloy's, is a catch-all for the kinds of issues outlined in the TASSC paper.

If you are committed to winning a short-term public debate with Astro Turf groups and industry-funded science commentators like Fred Singer, it helps if their messages have an element of *truthiness*—a word coined by the comedian Stephen Colbert to describe things that sound true intuitively, things that you *feel* are true regardless of whether they are backed up by evidence or actual facts. George Orwell called it "bellyfeel."

There is a great example from a Canadian climate change "skeptic" named Tim Ball, a self-styled expert, who often says that the Weather Channel can't tell you what the weather's going to be like next week, why would we believe them when they try to tell us what's going to happen in 50 years? This is silly: It confuses weather with climate. But it still has a ring of common sense, a ring of *truthiness*.

The *echo chamber* is an age-old technique, based on the assumption that if you repeat something often enough, people will come to believe that it is true. The painful example here might be the Bush administration's sales campaign for the war on Iraq which turned out to be a tissue of lies and overstatements about the likelihood that Saddam Hussein had weapons of mass destruction. If you go back in the record, you can see that every senior spokesperson in the Bush administration repeated this claim, again and again. It probably started as a Sunday morning aside on *Meet the Press.* Then it was repeated by everyone from low-level functionaries chatting idly with reporters to Vice President Cheney and, finally, President Bush himself. Then-Secretary of State Colin Powell, probably the most credible (and apolitical) person in the crowd, even took the argument to the United Nations. After that, right-wing bloggers, reactionary talk show hosts, and mainstream news media picked up and rebroadcast the allegations again and again. Only later, when the war was in full flight, did the truth come out. There were no weapons—and there had *never* been compelling "intelligence" to suggest otherwise.

Priming the echo chamber is easier than ever in the age of the Internet. You can salt a story in a small website or—if you are Exxon Mobil—you invest in "think tanks" that specialize in searching out favorable information and spreading it around.

One of the really great examples of the echo chamber at work was revealed in a book called *Heat,* written by the British author and *Guardian* columnist George Monbiot. When Monbiot was researching climate change a couple of years ago, he found a letter by the former U.K. environmentalist David Bellamy in *New Scientist* magazine. Bellamy reported that "555 of all the 625 glaciers under observation by the World Glacier Monitoring Service in Zurich have been **growing** since 1980." This would be significant if it were true. But when Monbiot phoned the World Glacier Monitoring Service, they said, indelicately, that the story was "complete bullshit." Glaciers are retreating around the world.

Monbiot chased all over in search of a source of Bellamy's erroneous information. The claim appeared dozens of times in many different locations—but all trails led back to the Science and Environmental Policy Project website of the aforementioned Dr. S. Fred Singer. When one of Monbiot's associates called Singer, he lashed out, saying Monbiot "has been smoking something or other." But Singer later conceded that the information *had* originated on his site. He said it was posted there by "former SEPP associate Candace Crandall." Singer acknowledged that the information "appears to be incorrect and has been updated." But 18 months later, it was still posted on his site, misleading people as it bounced around the Internet—being picked up in speeches and mainstream media.

Singer also failed to mention that he has a personal relationship with the *former* associate, Candace Crandall: She's his wife.

As an aside, Greenpeace's *Exxon Secrets* reports that Fred Singer is on the payroll of at least 15 of the Exxon-sponsored think tanks. It's hard, again, to imagine that this "coordinated local activism" is, by any reasonable definition, of the "grassroots" variety.

As Tom Harris of the ICSC pointed out, another aspect of the echo chamber technique is the ease with which a well-funded, well-organized group can influence mainstream media. The technique Harris was suggesting is relatively simple: Make a certain selection of articles or opinions widely available, and then encourage or harass editors—as appropriate—to see they get placed.

In the modern media world, this kind of manipulation is easier than it should be. As the pace of life becomes quicker—and as the issues become more complex—reporters have to work ever harder to keep current and to keep ahead of the competition. Accordingly, every newsroom relies to a surprising extent on legions of public relations people who provide story ideas and who—in many cases—do a lot of the legwork for which reporters don't always have time. People on both sides of the media/PR divide recognize the complications of this relationship, and the good ones respect the goals, the duties, and the responsibilities of their counterpart.

Most reporters still harbor a healthy skepticism of everything that comes directly from a professional communicator. But they don't always show the same wariness when dealing with people whose self-interest is not as clear. So someone like Harris, who shows up with a well-crafted argument, a "think tank" report, and no obvious[1] corporate links, gets taken much more seriously than he deserves.

Thanks, again, to reporters' general state of overwork, it is also easier to confuse or mislead people as the issues in question grow more complex. In all but the biggest news outlets, reporters are simply too busy to gain expertise in every issue that they are asked to cover. They are reduced to relying on "experts" and they often cover themselves by quoting experts on both sides of any issue they know will be contentious.

This "two-sides-to-every-story" approach is, perhaps, appropriate when you are talking about public policy issues or issues of morality—issues like abortion where the alternative positions sometimes rest on ethical conviction rather than on science. But on a science matter that can be demonstrated as clearly as the effect of CO_2 on global climate, reporters have a responsibility to inform themselves. They particularly have a duty to weigh carefully the relative credibility, qualifications, experience, and motivations of their chosen sources—a duty they too often forego.

A fair amount of serious academic research has been conducted on this phenomenon as it applies to the climate change "debate." For example, Dr. Naomi Oreskes, a professor of history and scientific studies at U.C. San Diego, conducted a formal review in 2003 of this "debate" as it appeared in the scientific literature, where new material is based on clearly stated evidence and accepted scientific method and where all articles must stand up to peer review. Oreskes took a random selection of abstracts for 928 climate change-related journal articles that appeared

---

1 Harris stumbled onto the public stage in 2006 as a tout for a Canadian group called the Friends of Science, an "independent organization" that was later shown to be funded almost entirely by Canadian oil and gas companies. Harris then moved on, creating something called the Natural Resources Stewardship Project (NRSP), another "independent" organization that, we later learned, was created at the behest of a firm of Toronto lobbyists who specialize in energy issues. It has not yet emerged who is funding Harris's most recent "independent" organization, the International Climate Science Coalition, but his list of "experts" include virtually everyone associated with the "Friends" and the NRSP.

between 1993 and 2003, and she found that not a single peer-reviewed journal article challenged the scientific consensus that human activity is causing climate change. Some supported the consensus directly, some by implication, and some didn't comment one way or the other. But *none* took issue with the position that human activity is causing the planet to warm at a pace unprecedented in human history.

So, that's what was happening in the serious scientific literature. How was that reflected in mainstream media? Two other academic researchers, the brothers Max and Jules Boykoff, conducted an exhaustive survey of what they called the "prestige press"—the *New York Times*, *Wall Street Journal*, *Washington Post*, and *Los Angeles Times*—between 1998 and 2002.

They found that in 53 percent of the stories, reporters gave ink to one "expert" affirming that climate change is a problem, and one "expert" denying it. And in a further six percent of the stories, reporters quoted only "experts" who were arguing that there was no warming or that any warming that had occurred was unrelated to human activity. So while "scientists" like Fred Singer were conducting no research and publishing nothing in the professional journals, they were still being quoted in almost 60 percent of all mainstream newspaper stories. And this sample was taken in four of America's biggest papers—journals of record that had sufficient staff to employ science and environmental specialists. No matter how hard it may ultimately be on their reputation, the people who are running this campaign have been enjoying stunning success.

And no wonder: They have had some advice that was, objectively, of very high quality, even if it didn't appear to be rooted very deeply in integrity. A defining example, in the annals of the George W. Bush administration, is something that has come to be known as the Luntz memo.

Frank Luntz is a corporate and political consultant and pollster, and a language specialist of considerable skill. In a 2002 memo, titled "The Environment: A Cleaner, Safer, Healthier America," which Luntz prepared for the Republican Party, he crafted a particularly slippery position on climate change in particular and on the environment in general.

Luntz began by admitting: "The environment is probably the single issue on which the Republicans in general—and President Bush in particular—are most vulnerable." Then he set out a series of points, of arguments, really, that would enable the Republicans to characterize their own position more favorably and to defend the interest of their major funders more effectively. On climate change in particular, Luntz said:

> Voters believe that there is *no consensus* about global warming in the scientific community. Should the public come to believe that the scientific issues are settled, their views about global warming will change accordingly. Therefore, *you need to continue to make the lack of scientific certainty a priority issue in the debate,* and to defer to scientists and other experts in the field. (Luntz's emphasis.)

Then, ripping a page from APCO's memo almost a decade before, he offers nine "principles of environmental policy and global warming," beginning with: "*Sound science* must be our guide in choosing which problems to tackle and how to approach them." (My emphasis.)

The whole memo, which you can find on the Internet by Googling "Luntz memo," is well worth the read. Luntz shows an advanced grasp of the subtlety of language and the importance of connecting emotionally (not rationally) with a large public audience when you are communicating on a complex scientific subject. His is, unquestionably, clever advice in a very bad cause.

For the record, Luntz's statement that there was public confusion was completely true, but the implication that there was "no consensus" among scientists was quite false—a position Luntz came to accept, publicly, without ever backing away from his manipulative memo, saying that it reflected his honest belief at the time he wrote it. But again, someone with Luntz's skill in manipulating language and opinions carries a huge additional responsibility in a case like this—especially when he is offering advice to the President of the United States. It is unacceptable that he should be able to excuse himself now on the basis that he wrote the memo without bothering to inform himself about the issues that it covered.

▼

No discussion of the dark side of PR would be complete without the mention of two names: John Stauber and Monsanto. Stauber is an activist writer and the founder and executive director of the Centre for Media and Democracy, which sponsors the excellent websites, PR Watch and Sourcewatch.

His interest in public relations was sparked in the early 1990s while he was working with another activist-writer, Jeremy Rifkin, on a campaign to block Monsanto from registering and selling rBGH, the bovine growth hormone that is now commonly used with dairy cows across the United States. Rifkin, Stauber, and many others besides were concerned that Monsanto was using its political influence, its wealth, and its PR expertise to rush into production a technology that had risks that were not balanced by the benefits. Early research showed that rBGH increased medical complications for cows and increased the amount of pus in their milk and many people are worried that, as a growth hormone, it may have long-term consequences for the children who drink the milk.

Early on in that campaign, Stauber learned that his own organization had been infiltrated by someone who was feeding information back to Monsanto. When other participants started to check their membership lists, they turned up someone named Diane Moser, who had identified herself as an intern working for the "Maryland Citizens Consumer Council." Further research revealed that no such council existed and that Moser was actually an employee of the international PR firm Burson-Marsteller—which made a certain amount of sense. The previous year, the Consumers Union, publisher of *Consumer Reports* magazine, had been working on a highly critical report on rBGH, when a woman claiming to be a scheduler for ABC-TV's *Nightline* called to request a faxed preview of the author's findings. Someone got suspicious, phoned *Nightline*, and found no one there who knew anything about the call. And when they followed up on the fax number, it rang in the offices of (you may have guessed) Burson-Marsteller.

Stauber got angry. "I started thinking, 'Who are these bastards and how can they do this?'" And when he got around to answering that question, he filed pages and pages of freedom-of-information requests, looking for information about Monsanto's dealings with the Food and Drug Administration and with politicians who had influence over whether rBGH would be approved for sale.

What he found formed the backbone of a book called *Toxic Sludge Is Good for You*, which Stauber co-authored with Sheldon Rampton. It's an upsetting book which should nevertheless be required reading for everyone with an interest in public relations, the environment, and in the manipulation of news and politics. When I read it myself, my first reaction was to recoil from its bleakly critical view of my profession. But the research was solid; the criticisms all well-supported. There really *are* a lot of people in the public relations business who are violating Edward Bernays' prohibition against putting the interests of the client above the interest of society—and doing so in a way that would breach ethical, if not always legal, standards.

As for Monsanto, it's a veritable case study for abusive and belligerent public relations. A chemical company with more than a century of dubious history, Monsanto got its big start with a contract to make the artificial sweetener saccharine for the Coca-Cola company. In a recent *Vanity Fair* feature, Donald Bartlett and James Steele point out that Monsanto then branched out into other food additives and pharmaceuticals and then into "plastics, resins, rubber goods, fuel additives, artificial caffeine, industrial fluids, anti-freeze, fertilizers, herbicides, and pesticides. Its safety glass protects the U.S. Constitution and the Mona Lisa. Its synthetic fibers are the basis of AstroTurf."

After years of trouble arising from Monsanto's production of toxic chemicals (PCBs, pesticides, herbicides including Agent Orange, dioxin), the company made an effort to spin off those liabilities into a new business called Solutia. Then, it re-incorporated "Monsanto" as a "life sciences company" focusing on agri-business and, especially, on genetically modified organisms (GMOs).

In this new guise, Monsanto has framed itself as an international leader in the global battle against hunger. Monsanto peddles Roundup Ready seeds that are impervious to its weed-killer, allowing farmers to buy both and, theoretically, increase production in the process. It sells, aggressively, its rBGH, creating a type of super dairy cow that produces more milk.

If you choose NOT to buy Monsanto seed and a few seeds from your neighbor's crop blow into your field, Monsanto can sue you for using their product—and sometimes win. If you choose NOT to inject your cows with rBGH and you try to mention that on your packaging, Monsanto lawyers are likely to harass you personally and professionally, while its lobbyists work to get legislators in your area to prevent you from bringing it up. The company is a public relations nightmare.

But Monsanto's belligerent, winner-take-all strategy is increasingly typical. Companies like Monsanto and Philip Morris act as if they are the champions of free speech. They suggest that, just as every accused person has a right to the best defense, every player in the court of public opinion has the right to put forth their own argument in the most aggressive and definitive way. But that legalistic argument—that adversarial paradigm—is totally inappropriate in the public realm. When two parties meet in a court of law, there are careful rules to ensure that the contest is fair. There are, for example, rules of evidence and penalties for people who perjure themselves before the court. There is also a judge—a trained professional who gives the matter his or her full attention—and whose decision is subject to appeal.

The court of public opinion is nowhere near as tidy. Most people pay little attention and many people bring little expertise. And while adversarial opponents often use a debating style that would have them ejected from most courtrooms, they often seem to be bound only by their own idea of what they might be able to slip past the sleeping judges. So, someone like Steve Milloy, who would be clearly identified in court as a paid witness for the Monsanto position, on Fox News is labeled only as a "junk science expert."

This unsavory manipulation has consequences. In a world in which cynicism is already rampant—in which public mistrust of government and industry is epidemic—companies like Monsanto and Exxon, and the PR firms they employ, drag down the whole of the public relations industry. They perhaps even endanger democracy, which rests on a substantial degree of mutual trust among members of the public. The Dark Side of PR could well be tapping the main vein into the dark side of the human psyche—at a cost that we will all pay.

▼

There was a story in the *New York Times* recently about Dr. Val Curtis, an anthropologist who is trying to get residents of the African nation of Burkina Faso to change their hand-washing habits—perhaps to save tens or hundreds of thousands of lives. Diseases caused by dirty hands—like diarrhea—kill a child somewhere in the world about every 15 seconds. It seems like such an easy thing to fix.

Despite years of effort, Dr. Curtis was frustrated to find that her public education campaigns were having very little effect. So, she turned for help to Procter & Gamble, Colgate-Palmolive, and Unilever, three companies with a grand track record of manipulating public behavior. These companies have grown rich by creating appetites in the marketplace for products that people didn't know they needed. And Dr. Curtis figured that people who convinced Americans that they needed disinfecting wipes, air fresheners, fabric softeners, teeth whiteners, and skin moisturizers might be able to convince her audience that they needed to start washing their hands with soap.

It was a master stroke. Representatives of those three firms jumped in and started to do the research, and soon found that people weren't buying much soap because they didn't think they were dirty. In rural villages, especially, researchers found that residents were very inclined to wash up after a trip to the city (always a grimy endeavor). But in places where modern plumbing had recently replaced pit latrines, they didn't think that going to the bathroom was dirty.

So, Curtis' new creative department put together a string of commercials and public health messages that put the "disgust" back into toileting. "Their solution," according to the *NYT* story, "was (a series of) ads showing mothers and children walking out of the bathrooms with a glowing purple pigment on their hands that contaminated everything they touched."

Once they stopped selling soap and started selling disgust, the hand-washing habit caught on across the country. Which is fabulous, except that it raises some complicated issues. If it is wrong to make good arguments in a bad cause, is it also wrong to use manipulative tactics in a good cause? What about a cause that is endorsed by a smaller majority? What then would be the right thing to do?

That last question—again—provides the key. There may be a thin line between manipulating the public for personal gain and using clever advertising techniques to save tens of thousands of lives, but there's still a big difference. In one instance, someone is working sincerely toward a public good. In the other, the public good isn't even considered.

There also is no way to resolve all of this by fiat—by government decree. We have experience enough with the downside of letting government make all the decisions about what is right and wrong. This is an issue that can only be resolved by the people who practice communications—and by the clients and members of the public who "consume" their services. PR professionals must rise to a higher standard. If you are in public relations, or you're taking public relations advice, you should ask yourself on every account, in every new situation: Is this the right thing to do? That's a tactic that isn't going to work for Philip Morris, for Monsanto, or, under current management, for oil giants like Exxon. If it's not working for you, then it's time to dust off the resume.

For everyone else, this becomes a time to speak up—to demand a higher standard and to vote with your feet and your pocketbook if you're not getting it. We have drifted into a malaise of public mistrust.

Only honesty on the part of communicators and activism on the part of the public will pull us through.

▼

This quote appears in the Wikipedia entry for John Stauber:

The *Milwaukee Journal-Sentinel* reported that, ironically, when Stauber was promoting his book on PR, it was delivered to the media with a slick press kit, and a prewritten list of questions for reporters to ask when interviewing the authors.

The implication appears to be that Stauber has committed some kind of offense by having presented his material in a professional fashion. It's as if Stauber's criticism of *bad* public relations means that he and all those associated with him should recoil from *all* public relations. I couldn't disagree more.

Public relations, practiced well and in good conscience, is a force for good. The whole goal is to improve communications and increase understanding between and among people. It's not an offense to shower, put on your best clothes, and arrive early for a job interview. It's not an offence to make the most of your relationships—to establish a good reputation and to submit references. It *IS* an offense to lie on your resume.

So individuals and organizations of all types should not shy away from PR. On the contrary, in the current atmosphere of mistrust, good communications advice is more necessary than ever. But we should all be wary of playing around the edges—of doing things that "seem justifiable in the circumstances." Ask yourself, as often as you can, if the thing you are about to do would make you proud if your mother, your child, or your friendly government regulator was looking over your shoulder. If the answer is no, then what you are doing is not "public relations"—at least, not as I would define it. What you are doing is making what will likely be the first of many mistakes.

Stop. Ask yourself: "What's the right thing to do?" The answer can only help.

3

The Social Media Revolution: Wedging Open a Window to the World

There was a time—perhaps only a decade ago—when the job of a newspaper reader or a television watcher was to sit still and listen quietly. Whether you were reading the newspaper, watching TV, or listening to the radio, it was like being in a really big lecture theater listening to the distant droning of a professor. There was, of course, *some* opportunity for feedback. Just as there are people in every classroom who sit in the front row and put up their hands—or who heckle from back in the crowd—the righteous, the disruptive, and the people who just wanted to be noticed could always write a letter to the editor. (And the newspaper could decide whether to print it.) But for the most part, it was pretty obvious that the professors didn't want to be disturbed.

That model may have been bad for the public, but there were elements of it that made life simpler for the public relations professional. The concentration of media power created a small, sometimes manageable audience for your efforts. If you wanted to disseminate a bit of news, you knew where to send the release. If you were hoping to shift the focus of a story, you knew which opinion makers you needed to convince.

This didn't necessarily make things easy. If the media gatekeepers were hostile, for whatever reason, it could become difficult to impossible

35

to reach the public. If your issue was not the flavor of the day—or if it only appealed to a small group—it could be hard to get any attention at all. And whenever you tried to engage the public in a dialogue, you had to do so through a media intermediary—usually a reporter who was more interested in telling an entertaining story than in advancing mutual understanding. As the cliché makers would often say, the power of the press belonged to people who were wealthy enough to buy one. If you could make that work for you (and your clients), good; if not, you were out of luck.

Those days are ending—overtaken by technological innovations and, especially, by the Internet. E-mail, blogs, Facebook, YouTube, Twitter, Friendfeed, MySpace, and the endless research capacity of the worldwide web have opened up the traditional tools of journalism to everyone who can afford a computer. "The old model was hub-and-spoke, where the endpoints were only recipients of news," says Norman Guadagno, a director of marketing for Microsoft. "The new model is that of an interconnected network. Now everybody is a broadcaster *and* a receiver."

This distributed network has allowed alternative public conversations to crop up all over, and on a nearly infinite number of topics. It has created what has come to be known as "social media."

According to Guadagno, social media has done more than just bust up the media monopolies; it has created an information revolution that is more profound than the social revolution of the 1960s. It has changed how we communicate and with whom. It has redrawn our social groupings—changed our physical neighborhoods into virtual ones. It has even changed the way we deal with one another personally, as we carry over the conversational habits honed on the Internet into our day-to-day life.

Jesse Hirsh, a Canadian social media watcher and consultant, calls social media an "engine for the anti-powerful—an authentic, interactive means of delivering content." He also praises it as a democratizing force; suddenly, he says, there is "a media option for people who weren't getting past the journalistic gatekeepers." The social media tools provided by the Internet "privilege expertise rather than access," Hirsh says. "In social media, you get power or influence on the strength of what you say, not because you own the printing press."

Informal but wide–ranging Internet conversations have also been increasingly effective at holding traditional power brokers to account. The best example is probably that of Dan Rather, the iconic CBS journalist who, in 2004, lost his job after an obscure blogger started speculating that one of Rather's stories (about President George W. Bush's Vietnam War record) was based on forged documents. Before the advent of social media, this was the sort of idle accusation that would have been rebuffed by CBS and ignored by other members of the clubby national media elite. But bloggers and independent researchers jumped on the story and ultimately proved that the documents really were faked. Dan Rather resigned in humiliation.

Where the public relations industry is concerned, Guadagno says that the advent of social media has created three major changes, each of which presents both an opportunity and a challenge. The changes are these:

1. Social media has removed a degree of artifice or "polish" that has always existed in marketing and PR. These days, Guadagno says, you have to spend more time dealing with the facts and less time on "positioning" or on carefully scripted "messages."

    That creates an instant opportunity to have what Hirsh calls a more "authentic" conversation with your audience. Companies don't have to worry so much about cooking up publicity gimmicks to get attention. They can spend less time on artifice and positioning and more time on the real narrative of their organizations. Rather than trying to squeeze points through a mainstream media filter, companies can use websites and other social media to make information available directly to their target audiences—and they can do so in full confidence that the information will not be twisted or rendered incorrectly by reporters who are agenda-driven, incompetent, or just confused.

The challenge is that whatever information you make available will be examined and re-examined, scrutinized by every interested party and from every angle. People with specific expertise (and their own agendas) will be checking to make sure that what you are saying is helpful and sincere, and not merely crafted to mask or control the conversation.

2. Social media allows companies to leverage the power of people who have not, until now, had a voice in the marketplace. Guadagno says: "For anything that we sell or advocate, we now can leverage the voices of our supporters, our consumers. We can take advantage of evangelists and activists." As an example, Guadagno pointed to the release of the newest iPhone, a product that Apple released with a relatively small advertising campaign and a unquestionably huge market response. Thanks to Apple's cachet and the anticipation that had built up for the iPhone, Apple's fans provided a type and amount of advertising that would have exhausted any budget.

    The opportunity here is obvious—at least it is to a marketing director for the world's largest computer software firm: It's great to have all that positive attention, and from a sector that was once entirely silent. It's word-of-mouth on steroids. The challenge, however, arises because Apple's detractors (and Microsoft's) have an equal ability to make their voices heard. If there is bad news, it will travel just as efficiently—and maybe a little more quickly—than the good.

3. Even aside from the chance to leverage testimonials, social media allows companies to vastly reduce their marketing and communications costs. Guadagno says: "We don't have to spend nearly as much on websites, PR and advertising. We can leverage an infrastructure that costs us nothing except truth."

    That last point is important. "You have to be able—and willing—to put out factual information," Guadagno says. "The cost of not doing so is immense."

This is the central "complication" for people who have grown accustomed to using manipulative PR practices. In a world animated by social media, there is nowhere to hide.

If you are spinning the truth, if you are burying bad news, if you have been using questionable public relations tactics like setting up fake grassroots organizations, there is a greater chance than ever that you will be caught, and that the damage done to your reputation will be devastating.

That won't stop unethical practitioners from trying to "hack the system," Guadagno says. And sometimes that will work: "There will always be people in the market who allow their voices to be perverted or paid for." But the success of manipulative tactics is likely to be short term, and reliable only in small group discussions where participants come and go and anonymity is the rule. Any disinformation that catches the attention of the biggest blogs or of mainstream media is likely to wind up under the microscope—to the distinct disadvantage of people who have been played loose with the truth.

The bottom line is that it's hard to tame an evolving environment and, by Guadagno's reckoning, social media is in its infancy, still evolving at a breakneck pace. "We're years away from there being enough stability in the system to allow people to take advantage of it."

There are some other good/bad aspects of the effects of social media, and especially of its distributed nature. For example, it is good that the Internet allows for communities of common interest to connect across great distances: No matter what your interest, you can type it into Google and come up with a host of buyers, sellers, or enthusiasts happy to join a conversation. The wonderful opportunity here, especially for savvy businesspeople, is the potential value of such "communities."

As Jesse Hirsh breaks it down, businesses in the traditional environment have generally thought about "markets" rather than "communities." But a market relationship is binary: A customer either makes a purchase, or not. Only in unusual circumstances do customers form a relationship that is more complicated—or gather in a community around a business.

There are two great exceptions that are physical, rather than virtual. Starbucks has created a whole generation of "clients" for whom coffee bars serve as a second home. While McDonald's was making its furniture brighter and more uncomfortable, to stop people from "loitering," Starbucks set out large, comfortable chairs and invited people to bring a book—to sit a while. As a result, Starbucks is now a "community center." It's made going for coffee a social occasion, a casual evening out.

The Canadian arm of the burger chain A&W did something similar in building communities of classic car owners. The manager at an A&W restaurant near Vancouver, B.C. noticed a group of older clients who were bringing their old hot rods for an informal gathering every Thursday evening. He welcomed them all with a free soda, and then told other managers about the potential. A&W started to advertise Thursdays as classic car night across the country, and soon A&W parking lots everywhere were filling up with people who know the difference between a "drive-in" and a "drive-through"—people who were delighted to "hang around" at A&W and spend some money while they were there.

There are, however, potential problems from the kind of social compartmentalization that is typical on the Internet. As people break into smaller and smaller niche groups—especially Internet groups that include members from many different geographic communities—it becomes harder to reach whole populations at once. It's not like the days when the daily paper landed on every doorstep in town or when everyone in the United States was choosing among only three network newscasts every evening.

On Guadagno's part, he says, "I don't even know what community means any more." He lives in a nice neighborhood and his daughter seems to have friends within walking distance, but the bulk of his relationships are conducted online, with people from around the world. Given his job, his nature, and his skill set, this is no particular problem for Guadagno, but it raises once again the problem of social isolation. This is not a public relations issue, but there is still a degree of social concern for those people whose only community is that of late-night gamers—or even early morning online bridge players, none of whom are going to notice if one of their usual participants falls down, hits his head, and doesn't show up for a few days.

As blogs and news outlets multiply, it becomes more confusing for the reader—someone who was, perhaps, already skeptical about mainstream news. Now stories and opinions are coming at them from every direction, forcing them to spend more and more time trying to weigh the credibility of different sources.

In response, some people gravitate toward specialized blogs or publications where expertise is obvious and easily proved. Others respond by moving to their social groups— ignoring experts in favor of listening to peers whose opinions they trust more. And still others seek news outlets that reaffirm their preexisting biases. No matter what the choice, this stratification makes it hard for businesses, social advocates, or politicians to reach diverse audiences.

Norman Guadagno also believes that the usual style of Internet commentary—of often-belligerent chat room "banter"—is weighing negatively on the standard of public discourse. "Everybody seems to be moving to a point where they think they can speak their mind whenever they want—that they don't have to worry about being civil. They seem to think, 'I can say what I want because this is the way I talk online.'"

This is unsettling but instructive, in that it speaks to the casual nature of the Internet conversation. Part of that is unquestionably obnoxious: People, protected by anonymity or, at the very least, removed from the personal contact that might rein in their excesses, tend to speak more belligerently on the Internet than in person. But *everyone* on the 'net tends to adopt a more casual tone, so if you are using social media—or you are helping an organization or a client participate in a social media conversation—it is important to set aside the old-fashioned corporate voice (which will only attract suspicion) and speak instead in a more human voice. If, at the same time, you are careful to maintain absolute accuracy, you may achieve Jesse Hirsh's definition of an "authentic voice"—one that people recognize intuitively and tend to trust.

Finally, there is the question of privacy—or the loss of it for anyone who is in a "public" position. Business owners, managers, and senior executives are becoming a new class of celebrity, often somewhat against their will. The Internet has made it easier to track people down, to monitor their actions, or find out where they live. Whether or not this can be turned to an advantage, it means that executives need to learn a lesson that many politicians already know: that if you want to be left alone with your family, you have to be willing to make yourself easily available in your professional capacity. For many people, this means developing a new skill set—it means learning to think and talk on your feet with much bigger (and sometimes hostile) audiences.

In most organizations, that's an education that must be extended farther down the ranks than ever before. Because even junior employees may wind up in casual (but written) conversations online, it's critical to distribute the skills that were once assigned solely to the communications department. Social media has made it impossible to maintain a single point of contact in any organization. It's best to recognize that, to make sure that everyone understands their responsibility and to give as many employees as possible the skills they need to do your organization credit.

If that sounds like risky advice (deputizing more people in your organization to speak publicly), ask yourself: What have you got to hide? If you come up with a long list, you should start planning now for the PR crisis that will arise when you are found out; you can be pretty sure that day will come sooner than you'd like.

The DeSmogBlog: A Social Media Case Study
Although Norman Guadagno warns that public relations firms should not try to "hack" social media networks, there is no reason that professional communicators should shrink from honest, active, and enthusiastic participation in whatever form of social media works in the circumstances.

Most large organizations, businesses, and public relations firms are already well engaged. Almost everyone has a website and the more adventurous firms have started blogs, opening up a public conversation —often a very lively dialogue—about their organization's news, events, and celebrations (and sometimes about their mistakes).

Four or five years ago, we at Hoggan & Associates started thinking about the potential for Internet communications. We already had some experience, working on our own website and on social media applications for clients, but there seemed to be a significant opportunity to add a public service element—something that would give us some social media experience at the same time as contributing to the public conversation on an important issue.

At the time, I thought it might be useful to set up a primer on climate change. I knew that the topic was controversial—and full of confusion— and I thought it would be helpful to offer a dispassionate and easily accessible analysis of the science. I started reading extensively and was surprised to find that the boisterous climate change argument featured in mainstream media was not reflected in the scientific literature. With a few outspoken exceptions, professional scientists were in easy agreement that the globe is warming and that humans are to blame; it's a position that, even then, was endorsed by every major science academy in the world.

Where, then, had I got the impression of confusion, of debate? The more I read, the more convinced I became that the public argument about climate change had very little to do with science and a great deal to do with public relations—and especially the unsavory sort of public relations that is giving the PR profession such a bad name. I started to get angry. I was personally offended to see fossil fuel and car companies investing so heavily in distracting the public from an increasingly urgent global issue. I was appalled to see communications professionals using their skills to confuse the public, and I started to think that *someone* should step up and start calling those tactics for what they were.

During the same period, I had also been looking at the power and the potential of blogs. They were originally "web logs," created as an interactive, online diary in 1997 by Jorn Barger, and shortened to "blog" in 1999 when Peter Merholz broke the word "weblog" into "we blog."

Over the next five years, blogs moved into the political mainstream and by January 2005, *Fortune* magazine was telling its readers that the business community could no longer ignore this new social media.

In mid 2005, we decided to launch our own blog, a platform from which to critique climate change disinformation. With a welcome investment from my friend John Lefebvre and with Richard Littlemore as the lead writer (at the time, the only writer), we set out to "clear the PR pollution that is clouding climate science." We launched in December 2005, at which time the blog-watching site Technorati reported that there were already more than 50 million blogs in existence. Our "blog consultant," a 23-year-old named Will Pate, was politely encouraging. He gave us a host of interesting pointers about how to set up our site and how best to court the attention of the major search engines. Given our specialized subject matter (and the fact that we had no intention of featuring nude photos or reviews of the latest in Internet technology), Pate said it was unlikely that we would rise quickly or far in the crowded blog world. In a best case, if we worked extremely hard and were unusually successful, he told us we might one day gain a Google page rank number of six out of 10.

Over the next six months, we set about building a readership, commenting not on climate science but on climate PR. Building on more than a decade of research by Ross Gelbspan[1], whom we recruited as our second writer, we began investigating anyone we could find who was disputing the science of global warming. We would check their credentials or try to establish whether they were working for the fossil fuel industry or for any of the many think tanks that industry supports for this purpose. Our results were stunning. Everywhere we looked, it seemed we were bumping into an organized (and provable) industry-sponsored spin campaign.

Our early successes were also welcome. Although we were not talking mainly about science, we were surprised to find that our early

---

1   Ross Gelbspan's books, *Boiling Point* and *The Heat Is On* were the first, best expositions of the intervention by the coal and oil industries in the public climate change debates.

readers were overwhelmingly scientists. (We could track readers' IP addresses and the overwhelming majority came from universities or research institutions all over the world.) Scientists contacted us to say they were delighted that someone was pointing out how politicized the science had become. Within that first half year, our Technorati ranking showed that we had cracked the top 2 percent of all blogs and by the time we hired our first full-time staffer, manager Kevin Grandia, we were one of the 12,000 most popular blogs out of 62 million.

By the summer of 2006, the DeSmogBlog had also become a popular resource for mainstream journalists. For example, we provided a huge amount of research assistance for a story in Canada's national newspaper, the *Globe and Mail,* which revealed that a Canadian Astro Turf group called the Friends of Science was financed largely by the Alberta oil and gas industry. We shared a scoop with ABC's environment reporter Bill Blakemore when we got a leaked memo from the U.S. coal industry drumming up funding to support the publicity efforts of another prominent "skeptical scientist," Dr. Pat Michaels.

By the end of the first year, we had reached what Will Pate had said was our full potential—a Google ranking of six. This is more than an idle marker. Google uses the ranking to decide how seriously it should treat your site, and how prominently it will display your content. If you have a higher Google number, the search engine checks your site more often and moves your content up the search list. As a result of our own good standing, if you search today for the name Dr. S. Fred Singer, a scientist who often speaks on behalf of industries like tobacco and oil, you will find that Singer's own website comes up Number 4 on the first page. In the Number 3 position is the DeSmog post dismissing a threatening letter from Singer's lawyer, and saying that we can report Dr. Singer as a liar because we have clear evidence that he has lied about taking money from Philip Morris and from Exxon Mobil.

The second year began with one of our sweetest scoops. The Intergovernmental Panel on Climate Change was about to release its Fourth Assessment Report in Paris, a document that would help the IPCC win a Nobel Peace Prize with former U.S. Vice President Al Gore.

We learned four days ahead of time that an industry-funded think tank called the Fraser Institute was about to release a counter report, an "*Independent* Summary for Policy Makers." We first found that input for the summary had been solicited from "experts" who had been offered money to criticize the IPCC report. Then we got a leaked copy of the actual report, which we passed on to some respected subject experts for review. The work was embarrassing—based on an outdated copy of the official IPCC summary and flagrantly ideological.

When we posted the leaked document, our traffic went up by a factor of 20 and we got calls from mainstream media from across the continent, especially from the U.K., where the Fraser Institute had scheduled a news conference three days later at which it had planned to release the report itself. They still had the news conference, but it was a lonely affair and Google searches in the ensuing couple of days revealed nary a story based on the actual report.

This was a best case in the circumstances—not that journalists continue to report on a phony science "debate" but that they dismiss the oil company PR campaign as a self-interested (and dishonest) intervention in the public conversation.

Thanks to the attention that we earned from stories like this, our Google ranking has since jumped to a seven out of 10—one point higher than our most ambitious expectation. We now reach more than a million unique readers a year, and our audience is increasingly dispersed, although there are still hotspots in universities, in Dallas, Houston, and Calgary and in the neighborhoods around Washington, D.C., and Reston, Virginia where the think tank crowd tends to concentrate. We also have excellent relations in our own communities of interest. We have connected with other climate change blogs and we regularly link to climate science blogs (and they link back). When we break a story like the Fraser Institute report, it is often snapped up by huge general interest blogs like Huffington Post and the Daily Kos, which reach millions of readers a day.

The DeSmogBlog is also a trusted information source and database for mainstream media. When Richard Littlemore and Kevin Grandia went in 2006 to the annual meeting of the Society of Environmental Journalists, they spent most of the time trying to explain to reporters what the DeSmogBlog was about. They may have gotten no attention whatsoever had they not already built good relationships with environmental specialists like Andrew Revkin at the *New York Times* and Bill Blakemore at ABC. But when they went back in 2007, they did so as presenters, running oversubscribed sessions on climate science misinformation and on the techniques of environmental blogging. The blog was sufficiently well known that journalists were seeking them out.

Having built those relationships, stories that might reach only a few thousand DeSmogBlog regulars on a particular day are soon picked up by online media and mainstream reporters for wider distribution—some days reaching many millions of readers. As a result of two such stories, Elections Canada is currently investigating the Friends of Science, trying to establish whether the organization illegally organized charitable tax breaks for its donors and then used the money (again illegally) to intervene in the last Canadian election.

This has been a bruising project for a mainstream public relations company—and especially for one that has worked extensively for resource industry companies. Colleagues, clients, and a few employees questioned why we would do something that drew us into controversy and why we would attract attention to ourselves as somehow environmentally aligned. Most often, I responded that I believed it was the right thing to do. I was outraged to see public relations people abusing their skills; I thought the public deserved to know what was going on; and I felt that the PR industry itself should be grappling with the problem, rather than waiting to react to outside criticism.

If my faith was shaken at any point, it was reaffirmed in 2007 when I gave the keynote speech to the Canadian Public Relations Society. It was a sharply critical speech—a direct attack on dishonest public relations tactics and an appeal for people in my profession to walk away from the business of backhanded manipulation. I wasn't sure how that message would be received. I knew that a small number of people had tried to have me replaced as the conference speaker. So I was surprised, at the end, to receive a resounding standing ovation.

The overall lesson is this: You should take social media seriously—extremely seriously. Despite the helpful input of our friends and volunteers, and including all the time I have put into the project myself, the DeSmogBlog has consistently functioned with fewer than two full-time employees. Yet, it is now listed by the *Times of London* as one of the 50 most influential environmental blogs in the world. And, at this writing, we had not yet celebrated our third birthday.

That means that a small group of determined advocates—or blistering critics—could just as easily make their way into your field of interest. This is a powerful tool, widely available. You should be ready to deal with it.

"Be careful" has always been good advice in PR, but never more than now. Watch social media. Don't assume a limited influence and don't stand by if you see inaccurate information. Demand the same degree of accountability that you would from a mainstream media source. If necessary (and if you can prove information is incorrect), you can even go to the search engines and have links removed.

A second lesson is that participating directly in social media, while risky, has the potential to deliver huge rewards. You want to avoid the pitfalls of cosmetic public relations, of trying to dress things up. To the degree this was ever effective, social media has rendered it obsolete. You also want to strive in all your communications to find an authentic human voice. It's hard to fake sincerity and perhaps harder to fake passion. But if you speak directly and honestly, people will recognize and appreciate your candor. And if you learn to use social media strategically, you may well be speaking directly to a larger and more influential audience than ever before.

The bottom line, however, is that if you are in the public eye—if there is any chance that you may become embroiled in a controversial public issue—you need an online strategy. You must be ready to deal with social media. Because when the revolution comes to you, you'll want to know what, precisely, is the right thing to do.

4

Once Upon a Time:
The Universal Appeal
of Storytelling

Pull up a chair. . .

With so simple a signal, we proceed into the fertile, compelling, confusing but absolutely essential communications field of storytelling.

If you interrogate your average dictionary, you'll be told that storytelling "is the ancient art of conveying events in words, images and sounds, often by improvisation or embellishment."

But storytelling is much more. Storytelling is the very essence of human thought and communication. Everything we know or do or say is, at some point, organized into a story—embedded in a narrative that enables us to remember and understand. And everything we see or hear is either folded into one of those existing stories or compiled into a narrative of its own. Stories provide context, a framework within which all the fragments have meaning. Our comprehension of "earth" depends upon the "sky." The notion of "mother" is insensible without "child." Even in fields of technology and science, where information seems to be transmitted in bits, stories rule. The concept of "five," for example, has no meaning without "four" and "six"—without "one" and "10"—without the whole numerical narrative.

Stories don't have to be long, complex, improvised, or embellished to still meet the definition. "I just went for coffee," is a very short story. It's not deep or compelling, but to a roomful of people who have been waiting to start a meeting, it might convey an interesting and relevant piece of information.

Here's the problem for the professional communicator (and sometimes for the misunderstood spouse). There are, at once, both too many stories and not enough. We live in a headline culture of story fragments and "messages"—a world in which we try to take advantage of a host of common stories in order to be understood more quickly. For example, our tardy meeting attendee (let's call him Carl the Communicator) might just as easily have said, "Boy, Starbucks must be rakin' in the dough," triggering in his audience a much more complete story. Now we know that Carl didn't just go for coffee. He went down the street, waited in a long line, and paid a great deal of money for a frothy concoction of coffee, (probably non-fat) cream, and incredibly successful branding. Using just eight words—none including the word "coffee"—Carl has told us why he's late, and at the same time revealed something of himself, his habits, his relative impatience, and his view of the commercial world.

What happens, though, if the audience is a group of recent immigrants from an Eastern European country that has yet to be overtaken by the North American coffee culture? The communication falls flat. What might have been a quick commentary on modern life—and a useful report on why Carl is late—becomes a clump of useless words, a story fragment that communicates nothing whatever.

It's like the old joke about the lazy reporter who was sent to cover the arrival of the Titanic, but who filed a memo saying: "No story. Boat failed to arrive by end of shift." Context is everything.

At the risk of taking an approach that is vaguely academic, it's worth looking at the foundations of the story—the history, the structure, and the relatively universal archetypes common to the human story.

Dr. Edward Wachtman, founder of the research firm, StoryTellings, says this:

Story is the *structure* that gives meaning and order to our lives. Instead of trying to make sense of the literally millions of independent events that comprise our lives, we intuitively organize them into an orderly sequence of events. We have a *past*, a sense of where we came from; a *middle*, who we are now; and a *future*, what we aspire to become. This is essentially the same structure—beginning, middle, end—that makes up a story.

Wachtman specializes in making or discovering iconic stories. He helps his clients develop the kind of unique narratives that will distinguish their companies and products in the minds of people who are busy processing "literally millions of independent events." He understands that good storytelling is the perfect antidote to information overload.

If you think about your own life, you'll see the evidence of this immediately. From grade school onward, the most effective "teachers" are always those who can tell a story—those who can put their information into a context that has meaning for their audience. The worst teachers tend to be those who are convinced, for some mysterious reason, that what they are saying is terribly interesting, even though they make no effort at all to explain why they find it so.

The first lesson, then, is to ALWAYS begin with a story. Always ask yourself: Where are you going (the beginning); how are you going to get there (the middle); and what is the point of the journey (the end). And then share that roadmap with your audience. If you don't—for example, if you show up to deliver a presentation with a PowerPoint deck full of factoids and no "story structure" for your talk—you will fail in one of two ways. People will get bored (fall asleep, check their Blackberries, chat among themselves) or they will tuck your factoids into a narrative of their own. They may leave with the wrong impression or with no impression at all. But leave they will, and at the first reasonable opportunity.

This is not just a question of being entertaining, although entertaining stories are usually the best kind. It's a question of being clear and comprehensible, of making yourself understood, even on those occasions when you don't have 40 minutes of audience attention. If your communication window is small, if you have no time to build a story in the mind of the listener, you still want to begin with a clear and complete story in your own mind. Then, you want to think about how you can tuck your message into a story that is already embedded in the common consciousness. Carl the Communicator hit upon a lightweight version: the "line-up-for-an-expensive-coffee" story. But there are bigger, more universal stories around and if you can tap into one of those, you have an opportunity to make an emotional connection that will render your story both memorable and compelling.

There is an old newspaper aphorism that says: "There are no *new* stories." After a while, every idea that passes the desk of the cynical assignment editor looks very much like something that she's seen before. But this isn't a new observation. The nineteenth-century French writer Georges Polti actually made a list of all the stories that had ever been told. He set out 36 "dramatic situations," ranging from action-movie standards like Pursuit, Disaster, Revolt, and Daring Enterprise; to film noir staples like Murderous Adultery, Madness, Mistaken Jealousy, and Fatal Imprudence. Polti said he was actually refining a list that he got from Goethe, who in turn had taken it from the eighteenth–century Italian writer Carlo Gozzi.

By the turn of the twentieth century, the Swiss psychologist Carl Jung was taking the concept of familiar stories one step further. Jung argued that the most important of all stories (he called them "archetypes") are hardwired into the collective human psyche. Jung said:

> The whole nature of man presupposes woman, both physically and spiritually. His system is tuned into woman from the start, just as it is prepared for a quite definite world . . . which . . . is already inborn in him as a virtual image. Likewise, parents, wife, children, birth and death are inborn in him as virtual images, as psychic aptitudes.

Jung argued that these archetypes, these psychic predispositions, create a kind of story template, provoking universal human behaviors and inspiring images, art, and myths of a sort that seem to arise in all cultures and at all times. These archetypes are the storylines that touch us at the deepest level.

The most complete of these stories is something that the American English professor, writer, and lecturer Joseph Campbell called the "monomyth." Campbell argued that the monomyth was universal, pointing out that numerous myths from disparate times and regions share a fundamental structure, including:

1. A call to adventure
2. A road of trials
3. Achieving the goal or "boon"
4. A return to the ordinary world
5. Applying the boon.

In a quote from the introduction to his book, *The Hero with a Thousand Faces*, Campbell described the whole process:

> A hero ventures forth from the world of common day into a region of supernatural wonder: fabulous forces are there encountered and a decisive victory is won: the hero comes back from this mysterious adventure with the power to bestow boons on his fellow man.

Campbell pointed to the stories of Buddha, Moses, and Christ as examples of this storyline. And you would have to add the adventures of Ulysses as described by Homer in the *Iliad* and the *Odyssey*. But a more current example is available (again and again) in the many-part movie *Star Wars*. George Lucas, one of the greatest storytellers currently working in Hollywood, is a self-avowed fan of Joseph Campbell's work.

The modern French psychologist and storytelling entrepreneur Clotaire Rapaille comes at the "archetype" (the foundational story) from a slightly different direction. Rapaille is a controversial character—a sort of commercial-era witch doctor who has made a name for himself by patching together a little psychological theory, a zest for marketing, and a willingness to work for pretty much anyone (for example, he proudly lists Canadian Tobacco in his website honor role of favored clients). But his take on the "story" reveals something about himself and, more helpfully, something about the companies that have learned to take advantage of its powers.

Rapaille argues that we all have unconscious associations for objects, concepts, and products. He says that *everything* has a "code" embedded in the brain—not just those things that were hardwired at birth. And Rapaille has made a great deal of money by convincing Fortune 500 companies that if you crack the code, you are one giant step closer to connecting with your customers.

Rapaille says these codes are burned early into the brain:

> When you learn a word, whatever it is, "coffee," "love," "mother," there is always a first time. There's a first time to learn everything. The first time you understand, you imprint the meaning of this word; you create a mental connection that you're going to keep using the rest of your life. . . . So, actually, every word has a mental highway. I call that a code, an unconscious code in the brain.

But Rapaille also credits Jung's archetypes as the most powerful, the dominant codes. It's part of Rapaille's theory of the "three brains."

We are all born with what Rapaille calls the "reptilian brain"—that instinct-driven personal computer programmed only about survival. Any archetype that rests here is destined to be dominant throughout life. In fact, Rapaille says, any sales pitch that appeals to the reptilian brain will overwhelm all the other stories.

The second brain, which begins developing in our earliest years, is the limbic brain, the emotional brain. It is here that we create what Rapaille calls the "imprints" for concepts like "love" and "mother" and "home." These archetypes are incredibly powerful, as well, serving as foundational mental connections that continue to serve as reference points long after the reference system itself becomes unconscious.

The third brain, which we begin to develop after age seven, is the cortex, the logical brain. This, in the commercial world, is where we consciously measure and compare. For example, it's where we assess the technical and economic benefits of a new car: Is it reliable? Does it get good mileage? Is it suitable to our needs? Rapaille allows that these are points of interest; but he says, convincingly, that's not how people buy cars. And for proof, he points to the Hummer, the archetype for which he "discovered" for General Motors.

In a 2003 interview with the PBS program *Frontline,* Rapaille said, accurately, that you can't sell a Hummer with a "practical" argument— and you can't believe the stories people offer when you ask them why they bought one. "Now, my experience is that most of the time, people have no idea why they're doing what they're doing. They have no idea, so they're going to try to make up something that makes sense."

Rapaille described that conversation like this:

Why do you need a Hummer to go shopping?
"Well, you see, because in case there is a snowstorm."
No. Why [do] you buy four-wheel drive?
"Well, you know, in case I need to go off-road."
Well, you live in Manhattan; why do you need four-wheel drive in Manhattan?
"Well, you know, sometime[s] I go out, and I go . . .."

And he concludes: "You don't need to be a rocket scientist to understand that this is disconnected."

So, Rapaille told GM to aim lower. He said:

The Hummer is a car with a strong identity. It's a car in a uniform. I told (GM), put four stars on the shoulder of the Hummer, you will sell better. If you look at the campaign: brilliant. ... They say (in one of GM's early advertising campaigns): "You give us the money, we give you the car, nobody gets hurt."

I love it! It's like the mafia speaking to you. For women, they say it's a new way to scare men. Wow. And women love the Hummer. They're not telling you, "Buy a Hummer because you get better gas mileage." ... They address your reptilian brain.

Another way to say this is that they appeal to your baser instincts. In an age of climate change—at a time, even in the mid-90s, when it was obvious that the American shift to larger vehicles was rushing society toward environmental disaster (and infrastructural overload)—it seems highly questionable to construct an advertising campaign that would entirely overwhelm people's better judgment. But Rapaille's success— amoral though it may have been—offers a stark illustration of the nature of storytelling. The least effective stories appeal exclusively to logic or reason. Only in the rarest circumstance can you win someone over with a superior argument. When you think about it, in order to get someone to accept that storyline, you have to get them to agree that they are poorly informed or just plain wrong. That's *always* a hard sell.

It's much more effective to tell a story to which people can connect emotionally, something that touches the cultural triggers or common emotions. But the best stories, the most compelling stories, are those that connect to Jungian archetypes that are common to all humankind.

A final component that you need before trying to construct any story is a thorough knowledge of the intended audience. People forget how difficult this is, partly because, in our private time, we most often gravitate to other people who share our stories and get our jokes. These are often people of similar culture and background, perhaps even similar intellect, and building stories for them is easy, especially if your audience members are readily accessible through conventional sources of media.

But that's not usually the case, especially for individuals or busi- nesses that are trying to connect with a broader public audience—with (prospective) customers or stakeholders of every type. Such audiences can be scattered geographically or dispersed by their different (and expanding) choices of media. They may be culturally diverse and socially disparate. And they may have vastly different levels of education or knowledge regarding your product or issue. Most frustrating of all, if you go out and ask them directly what kind of story they want to hear, your audience members may not be able to tell you. If General Motors had done a consumer survey before building the Hummer, it's unlikely that even their most aggressive female buyers would have asked for a vehicle they could use to frighten men.

So, in order to "discover" your own story, you must begin with a little research. According to StoryTelling's Ed Wachtman, you must discover the dominant Themes of your story and the Emotional Triggers. You must identify the Protagonist(s) and discover the Plot Structure. And once you have these elements, you must draw them together into an overarching narrative.

Sometimes, and with some stories, you will find the elements near at hand. You may know them already, intuitively. But if you are trying to discover the story of your company, your organization, or a particular issue or concept, you may well have to go to your target audience for advice. That can be a complicated process—especially when the archetypes that animate your story may be buried deep in people's subconscious. In those cases, you will need a process, and in all likelihood, the guidance of a professional—someone like Ed Wachtman.

The Sustainability Story—A Case Study in Research

In 2005, a few of us at Hoggan & Associates noticed that "sustainability" had risen in the public consciousness—not so much as a well-understood concept, but as a buzzword. Suddenly, it seemed, everyone was talking about making their product, their neighborhood, their corner of the country, or the whole world "sustainable." When we mentioned this phenomenon to friends and colleagues, we soon found that everyone had noticed the same thing: People (especially advertising people) were using the word more, but that it had begun to mean less. There were sustainable vegetables, sustainable sneakers, sustainable kitchen cleaners, even sustainable SUVs. We started to wonder, what's the story?

Actually, we really wanted to know two things. First, what was the true public understanding of the term? And second, how could we effectively engage public interest and understanding in a conversation about the concept? How could we get people to talk, to listen, and to care about living in the world in a sustainable way—in a way that would leave our children and their children with continuing access to the resources that keep us all healthy and wealthy (if not always wise)?

We were quickly encouraged in our curiosity. As we started looking for research partners, we found that there was widespread interest. Big corporations like Alcan and the Canadian Pacific Railway joined us, along with big educational institutions like the University of British Columbia, and, through the Globe Foundation, Simon Fraser University. From the public sector, we found partners in BC Hydro, the Metro Vancouver government, and the Port of Vancouver. And thanks to the generosity of the Lefebvre Foundation, the non-profit David Suzuki Foundation and the Fraser Basin Council also signed on.

For the research partners, we turned to McAllister Opinion Research for conventional polling, to ViewPoints Learning (see chapter 6), and to Ed Wachtman's firm, StoryTellings.

Wachtman is a student of the public psyche. In past work for companies like Ford, GM, IBM, and British Airways, he has sought out the details that separate relatively successful operations from what he calls the "storied brands" like Nike, Starbucks, Levi-Straus, and Jack Daniels, companies that have created what he calls "a brand story that resonates at a very deep, often unconscious emotional level." One of Wachtman's favorite examples is Harley-Davidson, a company that does more than sell motorcycles. The Harley story is a rich American tale of rebels and outlaws. As Wachtman says, in a paraphrase of something he heard from a Harley-Davidson executive: "What we are selling is the ability for a 43-year-old accountant to dress in leather and ride through small towns scaring people."

If you remember the female Hummer drivers whose goal was to frighten male pedestrians in New York City, you might think we are back to what Rapaille calls the reptilian brain, and you're not far off. Wachtman actually puts this deep emotional reaction in the amygdala, part of the limbic brain, but his larger theory of how stories work accords well with Rapaille's. Instead of referring to three brains—the reptilian, the emotional (limbic), and the intellectual (cortex)—Wachtman talks about Message, Meaning, and Myth.

In any story, the Message is top of mind, conscious, and public. It is about facts, attributes, characteristics, and opinions. It is rational, logical, and generally insufficient to carry a story on its own. The level of Meaning is more personal, more subjective. Meaning begins to touch the emotions and to play on the subconscious. But Myth is the most powerful level. Myth is archetypal, universal, and almost always unconscious. In order to get to the Mythical story, you have to pick your way through the thicket of rational thought, of explanations and justifications, and reach into the unconscious.

Wachtman always begins this process by assembling a field team, comprising key people from the client group. This team then gathers for a brainstorming session in search of two different kinds of story "prompts." First, the group looks for a single word that will get groups thinking about the company or concept. Then, they develop a short phrase that will provoke people to think more deeply about the subject matter.

In crafting this process for the Sustainability research, Wachtman also had an additional challenge. Unlike the usual corporate model, where there is a single company and, usually, a relatively homogenous market group, our goal in researching sustainability was to plumb the impressions—the similarities and differences—of two groups. We sought to learn about the attitudes and understanding of the general public, as well as the impressions and opinions of a smaller group of "Thought Leaders"—opinion makers and leaders who had been nominated by their peers and invited to participate in the StoryTellings sessions.

As it turned out, once the field team had designed prompts, facilitators conducted five separate, three-part sessions—three with groups chosen randomly from the general public and two from the pool of Thought Leaders.

Each of the sessions opened up with something Wachtman calls Word Play. Using the one-word prompt— "sustainability"—the facilitator launches a series of "quick-hit" word associations, urging people to nominate other words suggested by the prompt, and to identify those words as positive or negative. The session, which is helpful in building a vocabulary, as well as in understanding people's immediate reactions (whether "top-of-mind" or "gut-level"), elicited words like "environment," "green," "balance" and "future," and these words were overwhelmingly judged to be positive.

The second part of Wachtman's sessions, which he calls StoryTime, also tends to generate language that is common, and effective, in addressing the subject at hand. Wachtman began by introducing the second prompt—in this case the pre-selected phrase "working toward our long-term well-being"—and then he challenged groups of four or five participants to use pictures or images (some clipped from magazines, some drawn freehand) to create a pictorial story, a collage, and a narrative that would illuminate the group's understanding of that prompt. At the end of this process, each team got five minutes to present the story to the larger group.

In the third phase, Wachtman asked every individual to sit quietly and reflect upon their most memorable experience associated with the concept (sustainability) and to write that into as detailed a story as possible.

From all this play and reflection came reams of information that Wachtman then probed for meaning, searching for Themes, for Emotional Triggers, for recurring characters, and for a universal or common Plot Structure. What he discovered in the sustainability story was a meta-theme of "hope." Virtually every story triggered by the prompt "working toward our long-term well-being" rested most firmly in optimism. Wachtman also identified what he called Core Themes, and these appeared to flow directly into, and out of, a very consistent plot.

The Core Themes were Community and Interconnectivity ("we're all in this together"), as well as Epiphany, Transformation, and Reconciliation (hope). And the plot —one that seemed to recur in almost every story—was a variation of Joseph Campbell's monomyth.

It went like this:

1. **A Vague Sense that Something is Not Right:** The stories consistently began with a world out of balance. Despite our creature comforts, participants found that life seems a bit too hard, a bit too stressful.

2. **A Triggering Event:** While most of us go unquestioningly through life, in the sustainability story, the protagonist, the hero, hits a bump in the road, a wake-up call, bringing his attention to the notion that all is not as it should be.

3. **Epiphany:** This is the point of awakening, of recognition, or, in the monomythical version, the point of departure. It is here that the hero fully comprehends the challenge ahead and engages or ventures forth.

4. **Reconciliation:** What was broken must be fixed. What was out of balance must be restored and renewed. These are what Joseph Campbell described as "fabulous forces" that must be overcome.

5. **Transformation:** In the monomyth, the hero becomes somehow greater because of her adventures. In the sustainability story, that transformation may be mundane (someone beginning to recycle) or profound (someone resolving to live a fully sustainable, carbon-neutral life), but they are always transformed.

6. **Return and Responsibility:** Here again is the monomythical element: The hero comes home, rejuvenated, refreshed, and ready to act as a powerful force for change.

The assumption, in all of this, is not that you can or should try to create a story out of whole cloth. Neither should you try to contort every story into the shape of the monomyth; there may well be other archetypes that are more appropriate and, accordingly, more compelling.

The point, rather, is that primal stories exist, and if you can find one—if you can connect to an archetypal narrative—you will be much more successful in connecting to your audience.

In this process, we learned that, in the case of sustainability, that means acknowledging the complexity of the concept and grappling with the challenge of trying to find sustainable patterns in a complicated world. Even more, it means emphasizing hope, the meta-theme, and leveraging core themes like interconnectivity, community, and reconciliation. People already recognize how closely their lives are interconnected, locally and globally. They value community, and, given an apparently endemic sense of unease, they are eager for reconciliation.

People also move quickly to being part of the solution. Every small gesture that people make brings them closer to transformation, and once individuals commit to a more sustainable lifestyle (in whatever detail and to whatever extent) they become role models for their friends, family, and neighbors. They assume the role of returning hero, acting with integrity and sharing the benefit of their own transformation. They become the heroes in Joseph Campbell's monomyth.

The Sustainability Story—A Case Study in Practice

When we first received Wachtman's analysis, we all recognized something profound in his findings; but, at first, it was hard to put the information into use. Then we realized that someone we know well already had.

Ray Anderson (who sits with me on the board of directors of the David Suzuki Foundation) had written his own sustainability story with no knowledge of Joseph Campbell, no sense of being a mythical hero, and, originally, no clue even as to a ready definition of the word sustainability.

A Vague Sense that Something Is Not Right

The story began in the early 1990s. Anderson was drifting through another profitable year in a nicely profitable life. As the chairman of Interface, Inc, he oversaw the world's largest manufacturer of commercial and residential modular carpet and a leading producer of commercial broadloom and commercial fabrics. Yet, in spite of the strength of a business that he had founded in 1973, he was increasingly bothered by criticism—from employees and, especially, from his customers. People kept saying that he "didn't get it" on the question of sustainability.

And at the time, he kept responding: "Get what?"

A Triggering Event

In 1994, two Interface managers set up a task force to assess Interface's environmental practices and begin to frame answers. The managers asked Anderson to address the first meeting of the task force, precipitating something of a crisis for the CEO. Anderson says now that he didn't want to give the speech. He says that, at the time, he was thinking: "In my whole life, I have never given one thought to what I or my company had taken from the earth or were doing to the earth. I do not have an environmental vision. I do not want to make that speech. (When people ask me what Interface is doing about the environment), I cannot get beyond, 'we obey the law. We comply'."

In preparation, Anderson read Paul Hawken's book, *The Ecology of Commerce*, which argued that the industrial system is destroying the planet and suggested that only industry leaders are powerful enough to stop it.

An Epiphany

"I got it. I was a plunderer of the earth and that was not the legacy one wants to leave behind. I wept."

A Reconciliation

Then he got up, read the riot act to his employees, and set about pushing Interface to an impractical goal. "I made that speech, drawing shamelessly on Hawken's material and I challenged that tiny gathering, only 16 or 17 people, to lead our company to sustainability." According to a plan that Anderson calls "Mission Zero," he is determined that Interface's industrial impact will be environmentally neutral by 2020.

A Transformation

Interestingly, the corporate transformation has been all about profit. When Interface reduced energy consumption by almost half since 1995, it saved money. When it reduced the amount of manufacturing waste by more than half, it saved more money. When it increased the use of recycled material from less than one percent to more than 15 percent in 10 years, it saved yet more money. And the harder the company tried to meet its sustainability goals, the more popular it became, with customers and investors.

"What started out as the right thing to do very quickly became clearly, obviously, the smart thing, as well. The cost savings from eliminating waste alone have been $289 million cumulatively over 10 and three-quarter years. . . . Our products are the best they've ever been because sustainability has proven to be an unimagined source of inspiration and innovation."

Return and Responsibility

Anderson himself now spends a huge amount of time on the speaking circuit, telling a story of crisis and reconciliation, of epiphany and transformation. He is that rare thing: an evangelist with incontrovertible credibility, a man who can stand in a room full of executives and say: "There is no amount of money we could have spent on advertising that would have generated as much goodwill or contributed as much to the top line, to winning business."

He says: "This revised definition of success, this new paradigm, has a name—doing well by doing good. It is a better way to bigger profits and it cries out to be taught in our business schools and our engineering schools that will be training the engineers who must develop sustainable technologies of the future."

▼

You would be lucky, indeed, to look into your own life or your own business and find a story as resonant as Ray Anderson's. But (as Yoda would say), look you should. There is magic in there. There is material that may be useful in your public communications, and will surely be useful merely in understanding your organization better. You should know your own role, whether you're the hero who still hasn't left home—or the returning change agent who isn't getting the credit she deserves. You should know whether you should be selling fear (the Hummer) or hope (sustainability).

Most importantly, you should be constantly conscious of the importance of "story," the essential role of an organizing narrative that you can use to help make yourself understood. You will be doing yourself, and all those (perhaps sleepy) people around you, a huge favor.

5

Rewriting Reality:
How Framing an Issue Can
Help (or Hinder) Communications

"I've been framed."

This line is a crime-show staple, usually uttered by a guilty-looking character insisting that he has been thrust unfairly into a story *not* of his own making. In this version of a "frame-up," some vile trickster has constructed a phony storyline, a frame, complete with clues and circumstantial evidence, all of which suggest that our hapless hero is guilty. And the police, ever on the hunt for an easy answer and a quick conviction, have, metaphorically, taken the bait.

In real life, however, "frames" are not (necessarily) so terrible. If anything, they serve as essential mental shortcuts that help us manage information and understand our too-complicated world.

"People are not blank slates," says Susan Nall Bales, president of the non-profit FrameWorks Institute. We all have a set of stories and images already stored in our minds—evidence of a lifetime of "indexing," a process we use subconsciously to match new information to old interpretations. As the artificial intelligence expert Roger Schank puts it, "understanding means finding a story you already know and saying, 'Oh yeah, that one.'"

So, when the police are presented with a tidy set of facts and a guilty-looking suspect, they think, "Oh yeah, the butler; you can never trust those guys." The carefully planted evidence makes sense because it fits into an established narrative—a frame.

Frames can be like that: fully formed stories that repeat again and again. For the police, it's always the spurned lover or the violent act of revenge. But frames can also be metaphors—not so much a story, as a way to think about a story. George Lakoff, a professor of cognitive linguistics at the University of California, Berkeley, offers this example: "In intellectual debate the underlying metaphor is usually that argument is war." This metaphor then generates a whole set of vocabulary that affects how we think of what's going on. Instead of imagining thoughtful intellectuals, testing one another's positions and working to a new understanding, we see everything as an epic kind of struggle, to be described in the language of the battlefield:

- He *won* the argument.
- Your claims are *indefensible*.
- He *shot down* all my arguments.
- His criticisms were *right on target*.
- If you use that *strategy*, he'll *wipe you out*.

Susan Bales says a similar line of thinking develops when you characterize an election as a "horse race." The metaphor distracts people from the discussion of weighty issues and gets them thinking, instead, about strategy and poll results. Rather than being a sober exercise in democracy, the election becomes a game, where results are all-important and "gamesmanship" is not just expected, it becomes the central focus of the campaign. If journalists then add another frame—the adversarial, "two-side rule" in which opposite messengers are chosen to satisfy journalistic balance—you wind up with a blistering political debate, a metaphorical war that can only leave people thinking that politics are divisive and that the participants are disingenuous.

Soon enough, the frame can stop being a mental shortcut and start becoming a roadblock to learning something new. If we are always trying to fit information to stories that we already know, there is a built-in bias against "new" stories—against new interpretations of information that we think that we already understand.

In politics, public relations, or any other form of public communications, there is also a recurring opportunity to set a frame, to define the way people are thinking about a particular story. In his book *Moral Politics: How Liberals and Conservatives Think,* George Lakoff talks about the campaign by President George W. Bush to bring America "tax relief." This was a brilliant bit of framing—just two words that provide an overarching metaphor, an almost fully developed story. The word "relief" implies an affliction, suggesting that taxes are some kind of sickness or disease that people need help to overcome. If the Democrats opposed "tax relief," they would be seen as heartless —as unconcerned about the "tax burden" that was oppressing Americans. And if the President's opposition said that rich people didn't need "relief," they would be reinforcing the frame merely by repeating the language.

This speaks to how enduring frames can become and how difficult they are to change. Once an issue is "framed," once there is a dominant narrative or a widely agreed view of how to discuss and think about a particular issue, it is extremely difficult to shift the public conversation— to change the frame. The University of Michigan psychologist Norbert Schwarz demonstrated this in a piece of research he did on "myth-busting." In a major study that was later reported in the *Washington Post,* Schwarz tested a U.S. Centers for Disease Control (CDC) brochure that was intended to explode myths about the flu vaccine. The brochure listed commonly held flu views and labeled them either "true" or "false." Among the false statements were: "The side effects are worse than the flu" and "Only older people need flu vaccine."

Schwarz got subjects to read the brochure and then tested their recollection. He found that within 30 minutes, older subjects mis-remembered 28 per cent of the false statements as true. Three days later, they remembered 40 per cent of the myths as factual. Younger people did better at first, but three days later they made as many errors as older people did after 30 minutes. And everyone now felt that the source of their false beliefs was the CDC.

One of the explanations for this phenomenon has to do with the effect of repetition and the way the brain functions. When something is repeated over and over, it becomes more accessible in memory, and one of the brain's subconscious rules of thumb is that easily recalled things are true. It's true, in lots of cases, that easily remembered things are true, a fact that manipulators and spin-doctors can use to their advantage.

Given these results, the easy advice is this: Whenever you are likely to wind up in a controversial public conversation, make sure you get out first and frame the issue your way. Consider the story that you want to tell, the interpretation that you hope people will accept and the language that will support that interpretation. And remember that whoever makes the point first has a ready advantage over someone who tries to deny it later.

The Republican Party has grasped the framing concept well in the past, hiring linguistic consultants like Frank Luntz to conceive of frames that will resonate and "language that works." For example, in a 500-page briefing book that he prepared for GOP strategists before the 2004 election, Luntz noted that Republicans are particularly vulnerable on the environment and advised: "Therefore, any discussion of the environment has to be grounded in an effort to reassure a skeptical public that you care about the environment for its own sake." He then suggested that Republic candidates should spend a large amount of time talking about clean air and clean water, and he told them to avoid getting caught up in their opponents' stories about the necessity—and the past successes—of government regulating industry. Instead, he recommended that candidates say this:

> Unnecessary environmental regulations hurt moms and dads, grandmas and grandpas. They hurt senior citizens on fixed

incomes. They take an enormous swipe at miners, loggers, truckers, farmers—anyone who has any work in energy intensive industries. They mean less income for families struggling to survive and educate their children.

Suddenly, you have stopped thinking about PCBs flowing unregulated out of the Monsanto plant in Anniston, Alabama and down the nearby Snow Creek. You stop thinking about the sick and the dispossessed, about the ravaged mountaintops and clear-cut forests, and you start thinking about "grandmas and grandpas" whose fixed incomes make it difficult to accommodate social changes. It is a very effective reframing of an issue that many Americans thought they already understood.

That's a rare thing. Setting a frame can be quite easy; changing it, as the myth-busters at the CDC discovered, can be difficult indeed. But Susan Bales' team at the FrameWorks Institute has a theory and a method. The theory is this:

Most public discussions occur on three levels: "big ideas," "categories," and "specific issues." "Big ideas" include values like freedom, justice, community, and stewardship; "categories" are sub-groupings such as "the environment" or "child care;" and "specific issues" are most often the things that people have gathered to debate: clear-cut logging or child tax credit. But there is little or no prospect of progress if you try to argue about a specific issue. Usually, by the time that debate breaks out, people will have chosen sides. They will have decided what the issue is "about," and once they have accepted that frame, they will use whatever they can to reinforce their bias and then dismiss the rest as irrelevant.

The key, then, is to work up through the levels, returning the discussion to the "big idea" and trying to find areas of agreement. On the specific issue clear-cutting, for example, the debate is automatically limited to a question of "how" you are going to cut down a particular group of trees—ignoring bigger questions like whether or why. It is impossibly narrow ground, with one side insisting that clear-cutting is the most cost-effective and safest for the loggers, and the other side, perhaps, talking about horse logging or some other option that the clear-cutters would dismiss as impractical and naively romantic. Even if you bump up a category, to "environment," you likely will stay in territory where people's biases will prevent them from being able to hear new information. The very word "environmentalist" has become so politicized that it can start an argument at many dinner tables.

But if you engage people in a conversation about stewardship and responsibility—about the protection of natural resources and the preservation of some wild land for our children and their children—it is more likely that you will find common ground. Most people are committed to those issues, even if they have made social alliances with groups or industries that sometimes pursue conflicting interests.

Then, if you can recast a "clear-cutting" debate as an appeal for responsible stewardship, your audience might at least be willing to come to the table—to consider that their effort will not be wasted. They might even be willing to change their minds.

It's interesting that these three levels mirror the storytelling categories discussed in an earlier chapter. Ed Wachtman, founder of the firm StoryTellings, breaks issues into Myth, Meaning, and Message, and he advises that arguing at the Message level is generally a waste of time. Only at the level of Myth do people really engage with a new story, Wachtman says. Clotaire Rapaille, of Archetype Discoveries Worldwide, talks about the three levels of the brain: the reptilian, the limbic (emotional) and the cortex (rational), and he says that any argument that appeals to the reptilian brain—the most primal—will prevail over other emotional or intellectual appeals. There is a consistency to this advice, which suggests that different specialists are arriving at the same point from completely different directions. However you describe the level, it's clear that reframing occurs most easily and most effectively when you can move away from complex, highly detailed technical arguments and toward big concepts with broad and often emotional appeal.

Case Study: Reframing the Climate Change Debate

That begins to cover Susan Bales' theory of reframing; now to the method. Bales has been asked twice to study the issue of climate change, once in the United States and later again in a large project for the David Suzuki Foundation in Canada. In response, she led what FrameWorks calls a Strategic Frame Analysis, an effort to "understand how your issues are being framed by your opponents and in the media," and to use the best research in the cognitive, behavioral, and social sciences to help shift the public discourse.

For any such project, Bales pulls together a multidisciplinary team that can analyze the current public conversation, create a potential new frame, and then test that frame to see how easily it is understood in a broad audience and whether those who hear it actually accept it and use it as they think about the issue ongoing. In the Canadian research (with which I am most familiar as Chair of the Suzuki Foundation) we began by setting measurable goals for the research. We wanted to know how to engage a skeptical and apparently disinterested public in a public conversation about climate change policy—about what Canadians and their government should be doing to address the problem.

Having done a similar study in the U.S., FrameWorks was able to skip through its usual review of the literature and current public opinion data. It had already done a review of the literature and the recent survey material and it had analyzed TV and print and online media materials, so the preparatory research was largely a matter of testing the differences between Canadian and American audiences.

What they discovered is that Canadians were slightly less confused than Americans, but not really any further ahead in terms of taking action—or encouraging their government to take leadership. When asked about climate change or global warming, respondents tended to talk about impacts rather than causes and were mostly unable to identify human burning of fossil fuels or of carbon dioxide in the atmosphere as the major drivers. When pressed to offer a potential cause for global warming, the most common answer was that it had something to do with the ozone hole.

This was interesting information from the outset. In pondering why people are not taking responsibility for social or environmental problems, FrameWorks set out two potential answers:

1. People are selfish, small-minded and uncaring; or
2. It is a cognitive rather than a moral failure; they just don't *understand* what their responsibility could be.

In other words, people can't or won't assume responsibility for an issue unless they can take themselves seriously as an active participant in the problem—and particularly a participant whose positive actions may make a difference. When people don't know how things work, it's easy to spin them, to confuse them about their own role or about the responsibilities of government and industry. When they *do* understand, they become somewhat immune to the spin.

Having gained a sense of the public position, FrameWorks then brought forth first an explanation for climate change and then a "simplifying model" that people might understand more easily.

The explanation went like this:

> Nearly all experts agree that the average global temperature is rising, and that humans are causing this change. Experts sometimes refer to the problem of global warming as "CO_2 *Heat Lock*." Normally, the atmosphere allows excess heat to rise away from the Earth. By doubling the amount of carbon dioxide (CO_2) in the air we are blocking heat from escaping into space, and locking it into our own atmosphere. Heat just isn't getting out. It's as though there were a CO_2 Lock keeping the heat in. This trapped heat is raising temperatures and causing problems all over the world.

The simplifying model was considerably shorter:

When we burn fossil fuels like coal and gas, we pump more and more carbon dioxide into the atmosphere, and this build-up creates a blanket effect, trapping in heat around the world.

Then in a series of focus groups and national surveys, FrameWorks tested the effect of the model and of a whole set of messages—and messengers—who might reasonably be expected to lead public opinion on this issue.

There were a host of interesting findings. For example, if a scientist speaks publicly about the potential negative effects of climate change, people listen closely and take the information seriously. When an environmentalist speaks up to offer solutions, people again listen attentively and react appreciatively. But when an environmentalist talks about the potential negative effects, people turn off, dismissing the "Chicken Little" warnings as typical—and not credible—scolding from the environmental community.

In other words, different people are evoking different frames in the mind of the audience.

All of the lessons in storytelling and framing seem to come back to the same issue. First, people are overwhelmed with information and are constantly using a variety of techniques—conscious and subconscious—to organize information and to understand their surroundings. In order to speak to someone effectively, it is important to take this into account—to think about the social, cultural, and informational influences that may have colored your audiences ability to hear your point.

The second issue is that most people realize, consciously and subconsciously, that they have been played in the past. They know that politicians have lied, corporations have dissembled, and public advocacy groups have often overstated their positions. They know that the media is imperfect in the best cases and dishonest in the worst. That has left the vast majority of people skeptical, if not cynical. It has made it harder and harder to get people's attention; and when you do, the sorry history of public manipulation makes it harder still to connect.

That creates a greater challenge for professional communicators. As the research shows, public relations people have got caught in their own frame—a widespread public perception that PR people actively mislead the public on behalf of their clients. In order to change *that* frame, professional communicators of all kinds have to go back to big ideas, back to first principles—back to archetypal stories that resonate in the reptilian brain. Most of all, we have to ensure that we are telling the truth—all the time. If we do, people will continue to think positive thoughts about big ideas. If we do not, the public will withdraw further from our business and our clients, and no one will win.

The best chance of changing that single, big credibility frame is to establish a reputation for doing the right thing.

Source: Frameworks Institute: Changing the Public Conversation about Social Problems/Issue 8: Topic: A Five minute Refresher Course in Framing http://www.frameworksinstitute.org/ezine8.htm

6

Dialogue: Successful Conversations, Even Public Conversations, Have to Go Two Ways

In the communications business—probably in *all* businesses—there is nothing quite as frustrating as someone who just won't listen. We all know the type. Individually, they arrive at faulty conclusions on the basis of suspect or mysterious data and then they defend their position ferociously. No amount of new information—no argument, no matter how eloquent—will overcome their certainty. It can be the same in groups. Great swaths of people can buy into a position or a prejudice, and then hold onto that view against arguments that any reasonable and open-minded person would find overwhelming. It can get to the point where the prospect of successful communications with these people can seem absolutely hopeless.

At which point, it's good to ask yourself: Who is it who's *not* listening? If you have concluded that your audience is ill-informed and unreasonable, what are the chances that you are addressing them respectfully and listening to them openly? If communications have truly broken down, what are the chances that it's because *no one* is listening?

In the belligerent world of talk-back media, this is an increasingly common state. We are a society in which everyone is waiting for a chance to talk and too few of us are listening in the meantime. And no wonder.

77

From Plato's dialogues to CNN's talking heads, we have nurtured the culture of debate. Of course, no one ever reaches a resolution on the nightly news, and no wonder. That isn't the point. The TV exercise is designed to entertain, to feature quotable "experts" who will fight for their side and, if well chosen, will reflect the opinion of a large group of viewers. The opposing "expert" will battle with similar intensity and, ideally, will give voice to the bias shared by the remaining members of the audience. When it's over, the TV host will thank everyone for turning out and invite viewers back for a continuation the next night.

This is a great way to stage television, but a hopelessly inefficient way to advance a thoughtful public policy discussion. The chance of actually changing someone's mind within this model is incredibly remote. Instead, the whole system tends to solidify the opposing positions—to promote retrenchment. It is equally unlikely that a public "conversation" of this sort will contribute to anyone fully understanding someone else's point of view. People are so fixated on individual words and phrases— so intent upon finding a weakness in the other's argument—that there is no time to look at the big picture.

This is what has led the psychologist and social scientist Daniel Yankelovich to advocate for dialogue as a new way of communication and a new way of understanding public opinion. And the form of dialogue they promote is different from the traditional Socratic or Platonic dialogues. In the old model, dialogue was all about debate—all about argument. In the original version, Socrates would interrogate his dialogue partner, investigating that person's underlying beliefs in search of some fatal flaw. But while Socrates' goal was to more fully invest-igate an issue—to actually achieve greater understanding—those who followed began to use this technique exclusively to pick apart the argu-ments of their opposition. The goal was no longer to understand; it was to overwhelm, to overcome the other person's failure to understand.

But dialogue, as defined by Yankelovich, is a different kind of discourse, a respectful conversation aimed at achieving mutual under-standing and mutual trust. In his version, dialogue allows people to connect at a deeper level, to actually get to know one another a little better. The point is not for each party to try to subvert the opinion of the other, it is for each to listen and learn—to try to understand one another and, if possible, to discover common interests and common ground. In these circumstances, any resulting change of position can be celebrated by everyone, rather than derided as a loss or a concession. No one "wins" or "loses"—even if one or both parties migrate to new positions along the way.

The two most important aspects to this kind of dialogue are discipline and good will. Participants must be prepared to set aside their old debating habits and follow what Yankelovich describes as the ten ground rules for dialogue:

1. The purpose of dialogue is to understand and learn from one another. Again, you cannot "win" a dialogue.
2. All dialogue participants speak for themselves, not as representatives of groups or special interests. (This is contrary to the television debate, where participants are chosen for their ability to represent interest groups. Once ensconced in the TV studio across the desk from someone whose position they loathe, the participants then speak *at* one another, even though their principal goal is to speak *to* the larger TV audience.)
3. Treat everyone in a dialogue as an equal; leave role, status, and stereotypes at the door. (This makes it easier to honor what is being said, rather than who is saying it.)
4. Be open and listen to others even when you disagree, and try not to rush to judgment.
5. Search for assumptions—especially your own.
6. Listen with empathy to the views of others; acknowledge that you have heard what the other person has said, especially when you disagree.
7. Look for common ground.
8. Express disagreement in terms of ideas, not personality or motives.

9. Keep dialogue and decision-making as separate activities. Dialogue should always come first.
10. All points of view deserve respect.

If you can actually follow these guidelines, Yankelovich promises a conversation that will produce a host of benefits. This kind of dialogue:

- Dispels mistrust and creates a climate of good faith,
- Breaks through negative stereotypes, revealing participants' common humanity,
- Shifts the focus from transactions to relationships, creating community,
- Makes participants more sympathetic to one another even when they disagree,
- Prepares the ground for negotiation or decision-making on emotion-laden issues,
- Helps bridge subcultures and clarify value conflicts,
- Expands the number of people committed to the process,
- Brings out the best rather than the worst in people.

The problem is that dialogue gets more difficult as the size of the group increases. The ideal model is probably the face-to-face conversation between two willing participants—two people who are listening, watching body language, and responding appropriately and politely. It gets slightly more difficult as you move dialogue into a small group, and it becomes harder still for companies, non-governmental organizations, or political groups trying to communicate with large stakeholder groups. In most cases, anyone who is communicating with the public must do so through the filter of media, making it hard to get your point across unedited and almost impossible to hear a response. The Internet has made it easier to disseminate information directly, but even public opinion polls and focus groups cannot adequately give you a sense of where the public stands on a particular issue and, even more, where people may be ready or willing to go.

To answer that challenge—to achieve the benefits of dialogue in larger, representative groups—Yankelovich and his partner Steve Rosell founded Viewpoint Learning, Inc., an innovative research company that facilitates what Viewpoint calls "ChoiceDialogues." These are intensive investigations involving about 40 participants in eight-hour sessions that feature a good deal of two-way learning and teaching. In crafting the ChoiceDialogues process, Yankelovich and Rosell recognized some of the weaknesses of polling and focus groups. Both are inclined to elicit responses that are "top of mind," opinions that are highly unstable and sometimes fairly misleading. Pollsters are also under extreme pressure *not* to affect their survey groups, which limits the opportunity they have to learn more about why people think the way they do and where they may be willing to go in the course of shifting their position.

ChoiceDialogues, on the other hand, are informed by a carefully prepared workbook that offers both a good deal of information on the topic in question and a series of values-based choices that may indicate the likely direction of peoples' thinking. The long time frame (24 times as long as a typical poll and four times as long as the average focus group) also gives participants a chance to work through issues together. It is a supportive environment in which people can change their views as they learn.

Case Study: People Making Choices About Sustainability

Hoggan & Associates was fortunate to work with Viewpoint Learning on our first Sustainability Research Initiative in 2005 and 2006. This was an extensive study on public awareness and attitudes toward sustainability, and it included conventional polling and two more innovative research techniques, StoryTelling (see chapter 4) and ChoiceDialogues. Financed by a consortium of large corporations, several levels of government and (through the generosity of the philanthropist John Lefebvre) a couple of non-governmental organizations, the project was a huge success, in part because the StoryTelling and ChoiceDialogues sessions revealed information we could never have gleaned otherwise, and in part because each methodology wound up supporting or expanding upon the conclusions of the other two.

In the case of ChoiceDialogues, one of the most surprising but helpful revelations was that people have a much more thorough understanding of the sustainability issue than we had imagined—that it was other barriers, rather than a lack of knowledge or conviction, that was keeping people from acting more sustainably.

We were able to get to this insight in part because of a half-century of research that Yankelovich has conducted on how large groups of people make decisions. As explained in his 1991 bestseller, *Coming to Public Judgment: Making Democracy Work in a Complex World*, people come to important judgments about complex, often gridlocked issues in a three-step process. The first step, Yankelovich calls Opinion Formation, in which people's views are raw and unconsidered but they are beginning to get a sense of urgency—a sense that they will soon have to address the issue seriously. The second and most complicated phase Yankelovich calls Working Through. This is when people begin to look seriously at their choices and wrestle (often unhappily) with the trade-offs or sacrifices that they might have to make as they go forward. The third phase is called Resolution. Here people set out and begin to act on their optimal choices, often hesitantly at first, but finally with certainty and reliability.

In the case of sustainability—when it comes to how well people understood the issues and choices that we must face as we move to a more sustainable environment and economy—we at Hoggan and Rosell's research team from Viewpoint both expected to find our study groups in the first phase, still wrestling with raw opinion. It seemed clear from their performance that members of the public have not yet embraced the challenge of sustainability, so we assumed, wrongly, that meant they had not worked through the issue in any formal way. But faced with carefully prepared workbooks, a series of difficult choices, and a dialogue that unfolded in plenary sessions and in small groups through the day, it was clear that the participants in all four of the ChoiceDialogue groups assembled for this project understood the issue very well. No one doubted that North Americans are consuming the world's resources at a rate that is unsustainable—that would, indeed, be devastating if the whole of the Earth's population began to consume at this same rate. As Viewpoints reported:

> Overall, the public strongly supported making sustainable development a much higher priority. They were aware of the costs of doing so, and they were willing to make considerable changes in their own way of life in order to bring that about, *provided that certain key conditions were met.* (My emphasis.)

Those conditions were largely that government, industry, and other people get on side. Viewpoint found that people were personally and individually committed, but they were completely skeptical that anyone else cares as much as they do. They don't trust government; they don't trust business; and outside of those who shared their day of dialogue, they tend not to trust one another.

We were fascinated to find *that* conclusion supported in all three rounds of research. In stories, in opinion polls, and in closely monitored dialogue, the issue of mistrust rose again and again; and Steve Rosell was not the least surprised. He argued that a world without dialogue is a world without consensus. People have all kinds of opportunities these days to answer polls, to fill out comment forms, or to attend "public consultation" sessions. But there is too little evidence that anyone pays attention to their answers or reads their comments. And too many public consultations are really just government-mandated sessions in which influential people stand at the front of the room while members of the public "blow off steam"—and no one ever has any intention of acting on the opinions that are introduced in the process.

People have lost faith, not just about their neighbors' commitment to sustainability, but on a whole host of issues. They don't trust industry to look after the environment, they don't trust the financial community to look after the interests of small investors, and they don't trust politicians to do pretty much anything. In those circumstances, Yankelovich has created another list—this time covering 10 Principles for Communicating in a Climate of Mistrust:

1. Effective communication in a climate of mistrust is 80 percent performance and 20 percent telling people about it.
2. Make few promises/commitments and live up to each faithfully. Performance should *exceed* expectation.
3. Core values must be made explicit and framed in ethical terms. Ethically neutral/value-free stands are seen as deceitful.
4. More is expected from privileged institutions.
5. Silence/denial/closed doors are almost always interpreted as evidence of bad faith.
6. No one gets the benefit of the doubt.
7. Anything but plain talk is suspect.
8. Honesty/integrity responds to a genuine hunger on the part of the public.
9. Noble goals with deeply flawed execution are seen as hypocrisy, not idealism.
10. It is not enough to talk the talk; credibility comes from delivering results.

Dialogue: The Next Steps

The Sustainability Research Initiative was a huge and quite expensive project, but while the ChoiceDialogues revealed fascinating information, they did not (and could not) deliver a communication panacea. The people who were actually in the room left with a much better sense that sustainability is a goal commonly shared in their communities. We were careful in the selection of our participants to ensure that we got a good social and socio-economic cross-section, so the success of the dialogue process was compelling. But there are still millions of Canadians—and millions more Americans—who remain outside the circle of dialogue. Mistrust, rather than mutual public confidence, remains the norm.

That leaves a challenge for us all—a challenge to scale up dialogue to a much greater extent. There is no ready model for this, no company, no template, no established mechanism for engaging everyone in North America in a respectful conversation. But we all can contribute to an improved public dialogue by listening more and judging less. We can speak passionately for ourselves, but not presume to speak for others. We can set aside our stereotypes and assumptions. And when someone says something with which we disagree, we can say, "I hear you," and we can avoid the temptation of adding "but I still think you're wrong." We can criticize constructively and seek common ground. We can seek resolution rather than victory. These rules can apply equally in our private and professional lives.

Companies can work much harder to listen to their employees, their clients, and customers, their shareholders, and their neighbors. These are all "stakeholders" and all deserve to be treated with respect. As Viewpoint has demonstrated, there are sophisticated ways to "listen" more closely, if you can engage a representative population. The Internet also affords many convenient and inexpensive feedback mechanisms (see also Social Media) that should help companies and other public and private agencies become more attentive to the opinions of their most important audiences.

The key—the single most important part of dialogue and the single thing that we can all do individually—is to listen. The more you do of that, the more eager people will be to listen to you and the more likely they will be to believe what you say.

7

Getting Your Way: Six Principles of Persuasion (and the Reasons You Should Use Them Carefully)

When someone on a construction site says, "Pass me the persuader," you can be pretty sure they're not looking for an expert in conflict resolution. But handy as an eight–pound sledgehammer can be in some applications, the use of blunt force has almost no utility in the practice of public relations.

In the communications world, sincere and literal persuasion isn't just a good choice: In some situations, it's your only choice. If you are looking for public support for any reason, you have to know how to put your best argument forward—how most effectively to connect with people who may have no reason to want to listen to you or believe what you have to say. Even in a work environment, where you might have a certain amount of positional authority, it's a mistake to issue commands rather than to urge compliance.

"Persuasion has a tremendous impact on performance," says Dr. John Oesch, an assistant professor of organizational development at the Rottman School of Management in Toronto. If employees feel they are being treated fairly—if they feel that you are listening to their feedback and that your directions are generally reasonable and supported with a persuasive argument—they generally will work hard and happily on their part of the task. But if you consistently demand performance from your employees without making any effort to win their agreement, Oesch says, "They will leave, they will complain, or they will sabotage."

In public or commercial relationships, the latter two options are generally not available, so people choose the first. They just leave. They may or may not snarl as they walk out the door, but they won't buy your product again or support your project, and you won't like what they say to their friends.

So, assuming that you buy this argument—that you believe persuasion is a technique worthy of your attention—what's the secret? At first glance, the ability to be persuasive can look like a gift. Some people just have it. They seem to charm and engage easily. People gravitate to them, accept their assurances and, often, compete to buy their products. But Oesch says that there is method to the magic, and he says no one has done more to identify that method than Dr. Robert Cialdini, distinguished professor of marketing at Arizona State University and the most cited psychologist in the world on the issues of influence and persuasion. As if Cialdini's own ability to persuade is in doubt, Oesch says, "He's the best academic in history at selling his stuff."

That "stuff" is evidence—based on research on what works and why—when it comes to the art of persuasion. And, actually, it's not "art," it's "science," according to Cialdini. In "Harnessing the Science of Persuasion," one of his frequent submissions to the *Harvard Business Review*, Cialdini writes:

> The research shows that persuasion works by appealing to a limited set of deeply rooted human drives and needs, and it does so in a predictable way. Persuasion, in other words, is governed by basic principles that can be taught, learned and applied.

Learning them the first time around was an interesting challenge. Cialdini, as you will see in the coming pages, read the existing literature extensively; but, according to Oesch, Arizona State's most successful influence peddler also took a sabbatical early in his career and went to work with door–to–door vacuum salespeople and with debt collectors. He watched people perform and cross–referenced their achievements to their techniques, and he came up with six principles:

1. People like those who like them.
2. People repay in kind (you get what you give).
3. People follow the lead of similar others.
4. People align with their clear commitments (it's hard to move people off frame).
5. People defer to experts.
6. People want more of anything that is scarce.

1. Flattery Will Get You Everything

In yet another *HBR* article, "The Language of Persuasion," Cialdini says:

> Back in the 1960s, the brilliant media commentator Marshall McLuhan observed that often in the realm of mass communication, "the medium is the message." I'm willing to claim that often, in the realm of social influence, the relationship is the message.

You'll see the evidence of that in the first three principles. The persuasive power of experts is spelled out in a principle all its own, but the persuasive power of "friends" arises much more frequently.

The first principle gets to this most clearly: People are more inclined to listen to people they like. Thus, if you are trying to convince someone of something, it's good to start by building a relationship. Find out what you have in common. Find out what you like about them, and let them know. And then make sure they know about the things they might like about you. And (though this part raises concerns) flatter, flatter, flatter.

The example Cialdini chooses to illustrate this principle is the Tupperware party, an event that is generally rooted more in friendship (at least in "relationship") than it is in commerce. A 1990s study in the *Journal of Consumer Research* discovered that guests were twice as likely to buy Tupperware when they truly liked their host. They weren't buying because they needed plastic kitchen containers; they were buying because they also wanted to be liked.

Any number of smarmy car salespeople have stumbled on this principle in the most unscientific way, and pursued it unsuccessfully. Sincerity is an important component in friendship; and if people see the warm smile turn off the minute you turn away, they will consider you a fraud, not a friend. But flattery, it seems, always works. In fact, Cialdini turned up a study in the *Journal of Experimental Social Psychology* that showed flattery to be successful even when the compliments were untrue.

But, as every credibility is easier lost than gained, Cialdini's overarching advice is "uncover *real* similarities and offer *genuine* praise." That's a good start.

2. Do Unto Others as You Would Have Them Do Unto You

This is obviously not a new rule, but it has applications in business and public relations, as well as in interpersonal relationships. The most obvious is in the potential for payback from organized generosity. The example that Cialdini offers is that of the charity that sends you a "gift," like Christmas cards or return-address stamps, with their request for a donation. Having received such a gift (even if some people may feel they are being manipulated), twice as many respond positively.

These again are techniques that are improved as they become more genuine. If, for example, you treat your staff well, perhaps by praising their efforts and offering small gifts on special occasions, they will be more likely to respond with good will: They will work harder, take fewer sick days, and only tuck into the supply room when they actually need a new pen.

In the public realm, you may increase your own ability to be persuasive by making it clear that you are listening open-mindedly to public arguments as well as advancing your own. As noted in the earlier chapter on dialogue, if people think communication is one way, they will soon turn off. If they believe that their own feedback is being taken in good faith, they will be much more likely to engage—and to listen.

3. All the Neighbors Are Doing It

Every mother has asked the question, "Would you jump off a bridge just because Johnny did it?" And, under their breath, most children have answered, "Well, yeah! If the water was deep enough."

People are social creatures and they align their own actions to those around them. So, if everyone else in your department regularly takes "mental health days," most people will soon succumb to the temptation, believing that to be the norm.

But this principle—Cialdini calls it "Social Proof"—is also a force for good. A great example is the use of "Blue Boxes" in communities that promote recycling. When neighbors are unaware of the local standard, they may or may not take care with what they recycle and what they throw in the garbage. But when they see all the other houses on the block putting the blue recycling containers out on collection day, they soon begin to fall into compliance.

Susan Nall Bales at the FrameWorks Institute often cites another example. When researchers were trying to reduce root damage in California's redwood forests, they actually made compliance worse by putting out signs stating that too many people were wandering off the trails. People came to believe that was standard activity. They may even have thought there was some benefit to be gained by leaving the trail and getting closer to the trees, and they didn't want to be the only ones missing out. When researchers rewrote the signs to say that "most concerned citizens stick to the trails," compliance went way up.

The other application for this principle is in the "testimonial." If you are trying to spread a difficult message—especially during a crisis, when your credibility may be in question—it's much more effective to find messengers in the community who can vouch for your position.

Coming back to the question of relationship, people often won't believe you, but they will listen to their friends and their peers.

4. Can I Get That in Writing?

As any 10–year–old knows, in any negotiation, it's always better to get a "maybe" than a "no." A "maybe" can be turned into a "yes," but once someone has said "no," they seldom abandon that position.

That's what Cialdini is referring to when he says that, for better or worse, "people align with their clear commitments." On one hand, it is extremely difficult to get someone to do something that they have previously stated they are unwilling to do. And it's even worse if they have made that commitment in writing.

On the other hand, if you can convince someone to endorse an idea, out loud, they are more likely to follow through. And if you can get them to write it down, you improve your chances by another order of magnitude.

There are two obvious implications here for public communications. First, if you are advocating for behavior change, there is merit to going step by step. If, for example, you were trying to get people to reduce their carbon footprint by 25 percent in five years, only the most dedicated of your audience members would be likely to make an upfront commitment. But if you could convince the majority to start using compact fluorescent light bulbs, you would be on your way to success. By agreeing to use the new bulbs, the people in question will have declared, even if informally, that they are now "part of the solution." As a result, they will be much more likely to take the next step (improving their home insulation, driving less or buying a smaller car, buying local foods, etc.). They will align their future activities to this new commitment.

The second point this raises in public communication is in the challenge of overcoming firmly stated opposition. If someone says, for example, that they don't believe in climate change and don't want to make any effort to fight it, you will exhaust yourself pointlessly in the ensuing argument. Unless you change tack. Your climate skeptic may be committed on the environmental question, but they may also be very interested in saving money, or in protecting their community from other kinds of air pollution that are also commonly caused by wasting fossil-fuel derived energy. If you appeal, instead, to their thriftiness or their concern about visible pollutants, your chances of affecting behavior rise again dramatically.

It is important to remember, here as in other categories, that if you coerce or extort a commitment, it can backfire completely. Cialdini invokes the example of a boss who insisted that his employees make a donation to a particular political candidate. The employees complied, but avenged themselves by voting for the opposing candidate.

5. Trust Me; I'm an Expert

This is almost a punch line, more than a principle, and it is most often used satirically. But the truth is that in a complicated world, people are always on the lookout for a trusted source for information—an authority.

Advertisers have known this for a long time, putting white lab coats on the actors in TV commercials so they look more credible when they try to sell antacids or laxatives. That kind of manipulation is probably what gave rise to some of our cynicism about other people's claims to expertise.

So it is important in the communications world to choose your experts carefully. It's also important to make sure that those around you are fully informed about *your* expertise. People too frequently take it for granted that their colleagues or members of the public are aware of their credentials or professional track record. Spell it out, and try to do so in a way that is informative and not boastful.

It is also important to be aware that this form of persuasion is powerful enough to arouse concern about its use. Some of the best evidence of that is the 1960s research done at Yale University by the psychologist Stanley Milgram. Milgram set up experiments in which he purportedly broke volunteers into groups of "teachers" and "students." When the students underperformed, he instructed the teachers to administer electric shocks ranging from mildly painful to theoretically dangerous to life and health. As it turned out, Milgram's "students" were actually actors. The shocks were never administered, but 65 percent of Milgram's "teachers" agreed, in some cases under significant browbeating by the "expert" running the experiment, to administer shocks at the 450–volt level.

Given the potential for abuse demonstrated here, "experts" and the people who use their testimony have an additional burden to ensure that what they say is true and in the public interest.

6. On Sale—While They Last

The final persuasive principle is that of scarcity or, as Cialdini says, the truism that "people want more of what they can have less of."

Here again, we have a principle that is well–known, but that can be better understood. For example, Cialdini cites research that shows people will respond more quickly and decisively to what he calls "loss language" when they learn about a scarcity. In the study in question, published in 1988 in the *Journal of Applied Psychology,* half the subjects were told they would save money if they fully insulated their homes; the other half were told they would *lose* money if they *didn't* insulate. The second half, responding to the language of loss, were significantly more likely to act on the information.

People who deal frequently with the media often use this principle when offering a certain reporter a "scoop"—exclusivity on a breaking story. This can be effective, capturing the interest of a reporter who might not be interested if the same story crossed her desk in the form of a press release that had been sent out to all news outlets simultaneously. But per the constant cautions from Cialdini, it is foolhardy to take advantage of this method, by using it too often or, especially, by promising it as an exclusive to one person and then making it available to several.

▼

If there were to be a seventh principle of persuasion, it might well be "act responsibly" or "always tell the truth"—even if that's not necessarily your first inclination.

"This is not to say that, as a group, business people are inherently unethical," Cialdini says in yet another *HBR* article, "The Hidden Costs of Organizational Dishonesty," which he co-authored with Petia Petrova and Noah Goldstein. "All other things being equal, most executives would unhesitatingly choose the high road.

"Except in hypothetical situations, however, all other things are never equal. In any organization, people are motivated by myriad factors—sales quotas, corporate economic health and survival, competitive concerns, career advancement, and so forth—which can easily override their moral compasses."

As a result, if you learn well the techniques in this section, in this whole book, but you forget the overarching piece of advice—to Do the Right Thing—you could well find yourself enjoying significant short-term advantages.

But before you walk that road, Cialdini bids you listen to the advice of Edson W. Spencer, the former chairman of Honeywell Inc., who once stated: "The businessman who straddles a fine line between what is right and what is expedient should remember that it takes years to build a good business reputation, but one false move can destroy that reputation overnight."

In the long run—in the interest of a healthy and prosperous business—doing the right thing is the right thing to do.

8

The Capers Caper:
A Crisis Case Study, Featuring
Research, Recovery and Grace
Under Pressure

In 2003, Hoggan & Associates won a Silver Anvil Award, the Public Relations Society of America's highest honor, for Excellence in Crisis Communications, Business. This is the story of that crisis, and the campaign that left a business with a reputation that was stronger than ever.

If you had asked the question on March 25, 2002, an objective observer—even a seasoned communications professional—likely would have told you that Capers Community Markets had no need of public relations advice. In its 17 years of operations, this chain of natural and organic markets in Vancouver (Canada) had built a sterling reputation entirely on its merits. A pioneer and innovator in the organic food business, Capers' markets were the outlets of choice for people who wanted fresh, local, high-quality natural and organic food. Its stores' aisles were brimming with customers and its restaurant and deli bars seemed always to be running at capacity. Capers had great relations with local food suppliers, especially farmers, and a great reputation in the community: The calendar was crowded with Capers-sponsored events. It was, all in all, a tribute to Capers' good management and its good fortune.

As March 26 dawned, Capers was still well-managed, but it ran fresh out of luck. The local public health office called to say that one of Capers' employees—a food handler in its commissary—had tested positive for Hepatitis A, an acute and highly infectious disease of the liver. Given that Capers' commissary provided fresh deli items to an average 40,000 customers a week, the Health Authority advised Capers (quite correctly) that it would immediately release a public health notice.

This is the kind of news that could destroy a business overnight. Capers' customers had been paying a premium to ensure that they were buying the best, most nutritious food available. And as the leading organic food company in the city, Capers had invited the public— and the media—to judge its performance by a higher standard. For example, whenever there was a food quality issue in the news, reporters tended to phone Capers for a response, and Capers was understand- ably accommodating.

Now the crowd of reporters exploded to a size that Capers had never experienced. Every TV and radio broadcast in town was running the Hepatitis A story as its lead item, and Capers' phones were ringing off the hook with calls of concern. Again, as an organic food retailer, Capers had been the outlet of choice for anyone who was immune- compromised or who had other health-related issues. Now, these people felt their health was at risk *because* of the effort they had made, and the expense they had incurred, to shop at Capers.

By the end of the week, Capers was swamped by the attention and at a loss as to how to manage the media horde. The company phoned Hoggan & Associates on the Thursday, and we immediately set aside any plans we might have had for a restful Easter weekend.

The first task for us was to make the case that we were the right PR firm for the job—that we had the right crisis-management credentials and the right ethical approach to crisis management. And it was not enough just to convince Capers. The company was owned by the Colorado-based Wild Oats Markets (since taken over by Whole Foods), and the owners were rightfully concerned about the effect this outbreak might have on Wild Oats' reputation, as well. That first teleconference set a wonderful tone. Our concern was that Capers would take our advice: It was essential if we were to protect the company's reputation that Capers make some hard decisions and make them quickly. You can't help a company that isn't willing to help itself.

But Capers and Wild Oats had concerns of their own: They wanted to be sure that we wouldn't show up with some cosmetic PR campaign to minimize the situation or to spin the media. When the Wild Oats executives in Boulder asked me to explain my approach to public relations, I said: "1. Do the right thing; 2. Be seen to be doing the right thing; and 3. Don't get #1 and #2 mixed up." They said, "You're hired."

Of course, when you lay it out like that in a theoretical discussion, everyone agrees that doing the right thing is a great idea. But when doing "the right thing" means shutting down your commissary for two months and giving all of your commissary employees a leave with full pay, lots of companies would have balked. Capers didn't hesitate. The incubation period for Hepatitis A is 50 days, and newly infected people become contagious two weeks before they begin to show symptoms. The only safe way to be absolutely sure that NO food-handling employee was carrying the virus—and passing it along—was to shut down and wait for the incubation period to pass.

Capers also agreed to issue a quick and complete apology for the inconvenience and potential health risk caused to customers—in full-page ads in the local papers. There is an increasing amount of evidence that timely apologies are welcomed by the public and respected by the courts. A quick apology can actually reduce damages in a case where a company was actually culpable.

In this case, we proved the effectiveness of the apology with a series of public opinion polls that we ran during the course of the crisis. The first poll showed that 98 percent of Capers' customers knew about the Hepatitis A scare and 88 percent thought that Capers was handling the issue appropriately. In the second poll, taken just after the apology, the latter figure jumped by seven points: 97 per cent of the clients we polled said they approved of Capers' management.

As already noted, however, good management without good fortune is sometimes not enough. While Capers was eager to do the right thing— for its customers and for the public at large—the fates seemed to conspire, throwing up one roadblock after another. As already mentioned, it was Easter weekend and the local Health Authority was already in disarray. The CEO had recently resigned and there was an ongoing labor dispute with health care workers. Accordingly, the Authority's public affairs staff was already overstretched, and there were no extra bodies available on an Easter weekend. This became a particular issue when Capers first tried to set up an information helpline. The Health Authority objected, saying that Capers was not qualified to give out medical information and that people should call the Health Authority's own Nurse's Hotline. We found out only later (from angry customers) that the Hotline was not staffed because of the holiday.

When the Health Authority set up a vaccination program, they did so in community centers that were not big enough to provide adequate waiting areas. Hundreds of people were forced to line up on the street, standing for hours in the rain and fending off reporters and TV cameras, while waiting for the opportunity to get poked in the butt with a syringe. When the Health Authority ran out of serum, Capers and Wild Oats volunteered to buy some quickly in the U.S. and to make it available in warm, dry circumstances that would not further inconvenience Capers' customers. The Health Authority refused, saying that the limits dictated by the Canadian public health system meant that the program MUST be run through the government, no matter how much longer, less convenient, or more bureaucratic that process.

Against this resistance, Capers continued to do everything in its power to show openness and to support its customer base. Capers employees provided food and water to people waiting in line-ups for a vaccination while we at Hoggan set up a bank of help lines and a website, on which we constantly updated information. We fielded 1,500 calls in our offices, while Capers took another 1,000 among its three outlets. Five thousand people accessed the website and 6,400 ultimately received immunizations.

There was never a question during those first days that Capers was putting the health and convenience of its customers first. But with the commissary closed and business in the food stores down by 50 percent, we also started to think about how to recover public confidence in Capers and its whole food products. From the very outset, we had maintained a completely open-door policy with media, allowing tours of the stores and kitchens—not once but continuously over the first few weeks. As mentioned, Capers was considered an industry leader and the media can be ruthless when they begin to suspect that a company has an overblown public image. It was critical that Capers' good reputation be translated into a bank of good will, for which it was necessary that Capers be seen to be acting both openly and in a way that was consistent with how they had acted before the crisis erupted.

We also worked hard to follow one of Stephen Covey's seven dictums: "Seek first to understand, then to be understood." We worked extremely hard to acquire (and then disperse) accurate information about Hepatitis A; and over the course of the crisis, we commissioned five separate telephone polls to test customers' mood, their understanding of the issues, and their attitudes toward Capers' performance. We used that research to measure the effectiveness of our communications and to keep our messages on point, adjusting when necessary to add information when there were issues the public still didn't understand. We trained Capers spokespeople and, especially through our hotlines, provided some expert public feedback ourselves.

After two weeks during which it seemed no one found time to leave the office, the crisis began to cool, but we knew it was far from over. We had checked with two other restaurants that had suffered food poisoning events in the previous few years in Vancouver and found that they struggled for 18 months before their business returned to normal. But even as we were trying to move to a longer-term recovery strategy, the bad news kept coming. Twice the Health Authority changed the list of foods that might have been affected—first reducing the list to exclude things like muffins (and denying vaccinations to anyone who only ate those foods) and then, after the vaccination window had closed, expanding the list again to suggest that muffins were in fact a risk item. People were enraged and justifiably so. Shortly after, the Health Authority announced that, despite the vaccination program, one of Capers' cus-tomers had tested positive for Hepatitis A. And then another. And then another. In all, eight customers were ultimately diagnosed, and each time the news broke, Capers was thrust once more onto the front page.

Yet Capers' continuing display of responsibility prevailed. It showed, by keeping its doors open to the media, that it was proud of its food handling standards and just as determined to raise those standards yet further. The first thing it did was implement a Hepatitis vaccination program for all food-handling staff. And in 264 print and broadcast stories, Capers consistently answered every question and took every measure to rebuild public trust. Within five months, sales were back to pre-crisis levels and in less than a year, Capers was exceeding pre-crisis forecasts.

The entire crisis taught or reinforced several important lessons.

1. An open and honest approach is critical in a crisis. Circling the wagon and saying "no comment" suggests to the media and the public that you have something to hide. But openness builds trust and credibility, and it gives you the best chance of fairness from the media.

2. Research is paramount: You cannot manage a crisis in the dark. Good research eliminates guesswork. The faster you can gather high-quality information about a crisis, the sooner you can get that information into the hands of a worried public, and the quicker you can get the story off the front page. There is nothing worse than the media discovering a new, incremental revelation every day, keeping your issue on prominent display. Research also enables

you to eliminate guesswork. If you know how the public is reacting, you can monitor the damage and measure the effectiveness of your communications. You can keep your messages relevant and your strategy on course. This is a short list of the research that Hoggan & Associates, in conjunction with Capers and Wild Oats, performed in the first two weeks of the crisis. We:

- Conducted four telephone polls to measure awareness, knowledge of Capers' standards, and perception of its performance, knowledge of Hepatitis A, and intention to change (or maintain) shopping habits.
- Reviewed 1-800 customer calls to evaluate quantity and type of inquiries, to assess customer perceptions and to revise public material when necessary.
- Reviewed briefing materials on Hepatitis A, on Capers' food-handling procedures, and on public health protocols.
- Met with store managers, employees, and health officials to learn as much as possible about how the crisis was unfolding and to plan next steps.
- Consulted infectious disease experts at local universities to expand our knowledge and understanding of Hepatitis A.
- Reviewed high-profile food contamination cases to identify best practices.
- Audited all media coverage.

3. There is no substitute for a good reputation. Capers was on excellent terms with the media, with its clients and suppliers and, especially, with its employees. At a time when it needed passionate advocates, every store clerk and shelf stocker was ready to speak up—to say that Capers was a good place to work and a good place to shop. You can't invent that kind of support and the media know it.

4. Always have a crisis plan at the ready. Capers didn't and survived, but things could easily have gone worse—and they could certainly

have gone better. With a plan in place, Capers could have responded much faster, preventing early confusion, saving time, money, and a huge amount of stress. With a solid plan in place, Capers might not have needed the best crisis communications campaign on the continent to weather the storm.

A final, broader lesson is one that has been proved time and again. Crises are a test of character. If you handle a crisis well—if you do the right thing and if the people *see* that you are doing the right thing—you can actually wind up improving your reputation.

There was, in this crisis, never a moment when Capers put its own interests ahead of those of its customers—never a moment when there was any debate about whether Capers was committed to doing the right thing. That being the case, it was an honor to work with Capers and with Wild Oats, to help where we could and to prove, once again, that in public relations, doing the right thing is the right thing to do.

PART TWO

Tactics: Hands-On Tips for
Everyday Success

9

Communicating Well:
Things Everyone Should Know

In business and in life, there are a few important things that you *didn't* learn in kindergarten. Here's a cross-section of public relations basics— tips that are critical for every communicator, professional or otherwise.

Don't Leave Your Reputation to Chance

Your reputation is one of your most valuable assets. You rely upon it to attract employees, clients, customers, partners, and investors. Some companies depend upon it for a social license to operate. That being the case, public relations—the cultivation and maintenance of relationships and reputations—is not a matter of ego-driven self-promotion. It's a matter of monitoring and managing an asset. It is a senior management function that, if delegated, should go to someone who has the necessary skill set and experience.

Credibility Rests in Good Actions, Not Good PR

Mistrust is often the obstacle to successful corporate communications. In an age of skepticism—if not outright cynicism—the public is inclined to dismiss corporate messaging as self-serving and therefore suspect. Communicating in such an environment is 80 percent about what you do and 20 percent about what you say. If, for example, you are trying to distinguish yours as a sustainable company, emphasize action and avoid inadvertently overstating your sustainable commitments. Focus your communications on specific sustainable business practices that others can measure and judge. Credibility will build slowly, but on a solid foundation.

Spin: When PR Goes Too Far

Every good communicator wants to present each message in the most compelling way. You highlight the good bits. You emphasize your point of view. But when you start leaning too hard on the facts—overstating irrelevancies or leaving out inconvenient details—that ceases to be good communications and becomes spin: Truth with a twist. It's sometimes tempting. If you sell tobacco, DDT, or CFCs, it's sometimes necessary. But it will bite you in the end. Long-term credibility is better than short-term profit.

Write Your Own Story

Whether preparing for a job search or a media interview, you should always begin by preparing key messages. These are the points (and the fewer the better) that are most important in the circumstances—the things you want people to remember when you leave the room. If you are not prepared, you are likely to follow your interviewer's agenda instead of your own, which might be okay in a job interview, but a disaster when facing a hard-hitting reporter. Set your agenda and stick to it. It's the best hope for leaving the right impression.

Write Clearly

In a 1945 essay George Orwell complained about the decline in clear writing and offered some tips that stand up well today:

- Never use a metaphor, simile, or other figure of speech that you are used to seeing in print.

- Never use a long word where a short one will do.
- If it is possible to cut a word out, always cut it out.
- Never use the passive where you can use the active.
- Never use a foreign phrase, a scientific word, or a jargon word if you can think of an everyday English equivalent.

Assume Intelligence; Guard Against Ignorance

Don't be too literal. When you are trying to explain a business challenge to the public, don't overestimate people's awareness of the situation. Assume people are unfamiliar with your issue and convey your point of view in a general sense. Be accurate without allowing yourself to get bogged down in the details.

Listen: It's the First Best Step in all Communications

Whether you're thinking about your customers, investors, or employees, the key to good relations often rests in paying attention—in listening. While not listening is at the root of most public relations problems, listening builds understanding, and responding to what you hear builds relationships. Always try to look for new ways to get feedback, and set aside the time to really listen. Conduct surveys, book tell-me-more meetings with clients or customers, have coffee with your employees. Just be sure that you know what your workers, customers, and investors think about you, your business, and your products.

Communication Is Always Better If It Goes Two Ways

At a time when the public suspects that business leaders say one thing but do another, one-sided corporate information campaigns can actually engender mistrust and, in controversial circumstances, solidify public resistance. The alternative is dialogue, a communication technique that gives your audience a voice. Dialogue can take many forms—on paper, online, on the phone, or face-to-face—as long as you engage in a two-way discussion. In dialogue, you listen and learn. You accept your stakeholders as partners. And, if you succeed, you recruit supporters with a real sense of ownership in your solutions.

Court Third-Party Support

The best compliments always come second-hand—when someone tells you that a mutual acquaintance has been singing your praises. It's the same in business: No amount of corporate promotion can match the impact of an unsolicited endorsement from a credible third party. Remember that when developing your communications strategy, and make sure that your best friends are also your best-informed friends. Speak well of those who deserve it and make sure your allies understand your business plans and, especially, the rationale for any unexpected maneuvers. You never know when you might need a good word.

Make the Most of Scarcity

When crafting a message, remember the power of scarcity. Robert Cialdini, author of *Influence: The Psychology of Persuasion*, says research proves what every salesperson already knows: Opportunities are seen as more valuable as they become less available. Just as people will pay more for the "last" waterfront condo, Cialdini says the scarcity mentality also affects management decisions. Potential losses figure more heavily than potential gains, and exclusive information carries more influence than information that is widely available. So, any time you can say, "act now or lose the opportunity," you add power to your persuasion.

Social Math: Making Numbers Matter

Statistics can add weight to an argument, or can sink it in confusion. The process of making numbers comprehensible is often called "social math." It involves breaking big numbers into digestible pieces. For example, instead of talking about hundreds of hectares of parkland, it's better to express the total as a number of football fields, a measurement most people recognize immediately. Instead of talking about gigatons of pollution, talk about how many cars it would take to produce that pollution in a year. Most importantly, always use statistics accurately.

Public Values Trump Private Facts

The famous American pollster Daniel Yankelovich points out in his book *Coming to Public Judgment* that you can't win a public argument with facts when your position offends the values of your audience. For example, no compelling collection of crime statistics will sell the public on free heroin distribution if most people feel drug taking is morally wrong. But, if you can make a complementary moral argument—for example, that controlled drug distribution can ultimately reduce drug dependency and improve public health—you will have a better chance of reaching your audience.

Corporate Values Trump PR Tactics

Organizational research shows that leaders in highly successful businesses don't fuss much about their image or about the latest headline: They focus instead on their own set of values and on what their organizations stand for. Staying true to your values doesn't mean you can ignore your reputation. While the leader sets high targets for ethical performance, communications staff should still ensure that a company is well understood and well regarded. But image will always follow performance. It's good to keep the focus where it belongs.

Never Ignore the "Elephant in the Room"

Being the optimists they are, business people tend to avoid speaking about problems and focus instead on solutions and benefits. Positive is good, but people won't hear what you are saying about solutions and benefits if they are preoccupied with questions and concerns. Worse, silence on a pressing issue can be interpreted as denial, bad faith, or incompetence. Good communications on a serious issue begins with straight talk about the problem and then moves on to solutions and benefits.

In Apologizing, as in Comedy, Timing Is Everything

There was a point, about halfway through his presidency, when George W. Bush finally admitted that he was "not satisfied" with the pace of America's war in the Middle East. The president clearly missed his moment. Admitting a mistake long after everyone else has realized it doesn't usually change people's view of your competence. In fact, if your admission is half-hearted—or too late—you can reinforce an image of haplessness. It's always best to apologize early, before mounting pressure limits your options.

Euphemisms: Saying It Like It Isn't

There is a common temptation to try to pack difficult issues or bad news in padded language. Ministries of war become departments of defense; nuclear missiles become "peacekeepers;" military drafts are presented as "involuntary call-ups." In the corporate world, news of layoffs is often buried in announcements about "right-sizing." Unless you are an undertaker (in which case, some people appreciate thinking that their loved ones have "passed away"), avoid this language. People recognize immediately that you are camouflaging a hard truth; you'll lose credibility and still take a hit for the bad news.

Never Depend on Spell Check

This is a reminder, more than a tip (and a reminder from which we all can benefit) that in the Internet age—a time when we are overwhelmed by the printed word—tiny typos and casual errors have become more important than ever before. Every reader today is challenged beyond human capacity to keep up. Accordingly, every reader looks for clues that tell them what's worth reading and what they can ignore. In that environment, any error will send your work, and your credibility, into the dumpster. So, check it twice. Your reputation hangs in the balance.

10

Framing the Message: Getting People to Think About Your Issue, Your Way

In all public conversations, context is critical. We are all the product of our own history and all audiences have biases and preconceptions. Understanding those "frames of reference" is the first step to truly effective communication.

Communicating Effectively on Complex Issues

In a media-dominated world, people are too busy to study every issue in detail. Instead, most people use "frames," mental shortcuts to form opinions about news stories. When they read, hear, or see a story, they take cues from the spokesperson and from any accompanying visuals to help them assess how the issue lines up with their own values and experiences—with their personal "frames" of reference. So remember, it's not just what you say; it's how you say it, who says it for you, and how easily your message aligns with your audience's preconceived notions.

He (or She) Who Frames First, Wins

When your business is under siege, you can't hope to control the situation without first controlling the story. The most effective form of communication is a compelling narrative that ties your interests to those of your audience. This is particularly critical when you're caught in the spotlight; it doesn't matter if you have the facts on your side if your detractors are framing the story—if people are looking at your company through a lens provided by your critics. So, don't just react. Start now to define your company's story. Then you'll be ready to frame a response within that narrative should something go wrong.

Four Communications Styles You Should Avoid

Here are four popular communications strategies that usually won't help change people's minds.

1. Confronting people with highly charged contrarian arguments makes people defensive, reinforcing partisan or ideological beliefs.
2. Explaining an issue in depth assumes you can overwhelm disagreement with information. Usually, you just overwhelm your audience.
3. Spinning involves taking a position and calling it something else in order to distract or confuse the public. It's trickery that often backfires.
4. Connecting to your audience is usually a good technique, but if you try to connect by acknowledging an erroneous public opinion, you may only cement that preconception.

No Audience Is a Blank Slate

There is a danger, in preparing messages for public consumption, of treating your audience as an empty vessel into which you can pour information. Given that people generally understand issues within preconceived frames, you must work to identify those preconceptions before you try to add information or, especially, change opinions.

The first step is research: Find out what your audience knows and how it feels about your issue. Then make your case, and monitor the result.

Good communications is a conversation, which always involves as much watching and listening as it does talking.

The Effectiveness of "Myth-busting" Is a Myth

"Myth-busting" is a popular, but risky, technique in public information campaigns. You set out an incorrect piece of information (e.g., only the elderly need flu vaccines) and then present accurate information in contradiction. The form is tempting: clear and concise. But researchers have found that your audience may incorrectly recall your message. Three days after reading myth-busting material, people may conclude that the myth—so forcefully stated—is actually true. So, use myth-busting carefully, if at all, and keep myths out of the headlines. The bold-face message should always be fact.

In All Communications, Accentuate the Positive!

Few things will tempt a smoker as effectively as a warning that says, "No SMOKING." Research shows that people are inclined to read over the "negation tag" in a statement and fix on the active word. Ruth Mayo from the Hebrew University in Jerusalem explains: "If someone says, 'I did not harass her,' I associate the idea of harassment with this person." Even if an accused person is later exonerated, "this (harassment) is what is activated when I hear this person's name again." So, don't forget, REMEMBER, stick with affirmative phrasing.

For Good or Ill, Repetition Equals Truth

In an age of information overload, memory specialists have discovered that people use subconscious rules of thumb for sorting facts from fiction. For example, people assume that easily recalled things are true—confirming the old adage that if you say something often enough, people will start to believe it. Recent research also suggests that once repetition takes effect, listeners will conclude that the information came from multiple—and reputable—sources. So, when communicating new information: Repeat, repeat, repeat. And when trying to dislodge misinformation, don't expect people to digest a correction right away. Your "new" truth may also require many repetitions.

Choosing the Right Messenger

When framing an issue, the person talking is sometimes more important than what is being said. For example, a corporate executive and a union negotiator might look uniformly self-interested in a labor dispute, where an injured third party (a worried spouse or a displaced supplier) might cast the story in a different light. Surroundings are also important: A story about homelessness might frighten or offend if it featured a mentally ill person rambling down the street; but the same person might arouse empathy and concern if pictured receiving his first hot meal in a week. Framing is all about context.

Reframing: Use "Big Ideas" to Change Minds

To change public opinion, you often must reframe an issue at its highest level. Most public discussions occur on three levels:

- Big ideas (values like freedom, justice, community, and sustainability),
- Categories ("the environment" or "child care"), and
- Specific issues (clear cut logging or child tax credits).

Your message must work at every level; but the high-level frame is crucial. Arguments for child tax credits, for example, may fail if people are stuck in a "freedom" frame, obsessing about government intervention. Ask them to consider it in the context of "community," however, and their sense of responsibility may trump their concern.

11

Courting Media Coverage:
Flirting with the Grizzly

Few public institutions are as powerful and attractive as the beast we have come to know as the mainstream media. But despite the ingratiating performance, the cuddly appearance—and the incredible value it can bring to your business—you should never forget the teeth and claws. Approach with caution.

Seven Clues to Making News

When pitching stories to the media, keep in mind these seven news values—seven elements that tend to make a story "newsworthy."

1. *Conflict*: Is there a struggle? And how high are the stakes?
2. *Humanity*: Is it a "people story?"
3. *Immediacy*: Is it fresh?
4. *Locality*: Are my neighbors involved?
5. *Celebrity*: Are there stars, athletes, authors, or politicians?
6. *Novelty*: Have I seen it before?
7. *Timing*: Does my story conflict with something more interesting?

It's unlikely you'll find a story with all these elements covered, but the more you can include, the better your chances of attracting attention.

Why Your News Release Never Made It to the Front Page

Competition! Media outlets receive thousands of news releases each week. But the paper covers only a few. Those that are picked up contain news that matters to readers. News releases that champion information suited for a company newsletter or advertisement should never be sent to a newsroom. Successful news releases also get to the point quickly; they don't beat around the bush. You can be sure that if you take three pages to say what you could say in one page, your news release will likely end up in the trash.

Great Publicists Are Great Listeners

The first step in attracting positive media coverage is learning what the media finds interesting and examining your company for elements that fit those criteria. Keep tabs on the headlines; watch who's covering what and track which stories are gaining momentum. At the same time, dig deep in your company for similar "newsworthy" details. When you find one and pitch a story, listen to the response. Follow up on press releases. You will enjoy much greater success if you study and respond to media interest than if you try desperately to sell your favorite idea.

Know Your Audience

"Find a need and fill it" is standard advice for entrepreneurs. It is also great advice for anyone looking for media attention. So, learn as much as you can about the media in your target area. Learn about their individual audiences and the kinds of stories they like to read or hear. Then be sure to address those audiences in your messages. Sharing your favorite steak tartare recipe with an audience of vegetarians is a waste of a great opportunity.

Invest in Media Education

If yours is a new company with complex issues or products—or an old company with new wrinkles coming up—take the time to tell your story to interested reporters, even when you're not in the news. It's best when arranging these briefing sessions to identify leading beat reporters, and to offer a senior officer of the company to conduct the meeting. You will build understanding and make important personal connections, so when your company is in the news, the leading reporters will be familiar with your organization—your product, technology, or business strategy—and will know who to call.

Media Kits: Making News That's Fit to Print

Media or press kits, while not perfect in every circumstance, can still be useful in garnering coverage for your issue or event. Be sure to include: a cover letter, brief and specific about what may interest a particular media outlet; contact information (phone, website, e-mail addresses) for reporters and, where relevant, for the public; a thorough, but not overwhelming who-what-when-where-why backgrounder; and a CD with useful images. Once assembled, call ahead to make sure you're sending it to the right person, and call again to follow up.

Keep Contact Lists Current

Media contact lists are invaluable—when compiled carefully and kept current. You should assume, however, that commonly available databases are out of date. So, before sending out news releases, be sure to confirm the identity and responsibilities of potential recipients. Then keep notes on frequent contacts: What stories do they prefer? How do they like to receive information? When DON'T they want to be bothered? By tracking reporters' individual needs you demonstrate that you're listening, that you can be a helpful resource, and that your press materials are likely relevant and worth reading.

Keep Step with Time

When releasing news, it's important to think about timing—to make sure that information and spokespeople are available when reporters need them, well before deadline. This becomes complicated on national stories when you're dealing with media in different time zones. For example, while it's tempting to give local reporters priority access for interviews, that could cost you coverage if you let West Coast media go first—causing Eastern reporters to blow their deadlines. So, make a national plan, and if you have to, give priority to those whose timelines are tightest.

Pitching News Over the Holidays

The holiday season is a perfect time to get news coverage. Newsrooms are short staffed and the organizations that usually generate news also tend to be deserted, leaving media—fat with holiday ads—starving for content. If you have a timeless message, well suited to feature treatment, this is your chance. But avoid looking manipulative. In the week before the holiday, don't hold back stories, hoping for bigger coverage. And don't try to bury something controversial or hide the notice of a public hearing. Most people are sophisticated enough to recognize the technique and may punish you for trying it.

Editorial Boards

INFLUENCE THE INFLUENTIAL

Got a story to tell, an angle the pundits are overlooking? Consider meeting with a newspaper Editorial Board. Most Boards consist of Opinion editors and columnists (and a reporter to keep things on the record). It's NOT the place to criticize news coverage; it's a chance to engage opinion-makers, to build relationships, so commentators know who to call when they address your issue. The Boards are busy: Expect an audience only when your issue is hot or when you have a substantive backgrounder on a story that will break soon.

GETTING READY

Once you have booked a meeting with a newspaper's Editorial Board, be prepared. The meetings generally last one hour and the best ones are spent in dialogue—lively discussion and Q&A—not monologues. Prepare an opening presentation no longer than 15 minutes. If your issue is so complex that you feel this is insufficient, send the board a background brief two or three days in advance. Finally, spend some time thinking about the hardest questions you might face: If you don't have credible, forthright answers that you're willing to give cheerfully, you're not ready.

THE BIG DAY

Editorial Board meetings can be collegial or combative; it's usually your choice.

- Be positive—complaining is counter-productive.
- Be specific—facts are good; rhetoric is bad.
- Be brief—leave lots of time for discussion and clarification.
- Be open—be ready to tell your story (warty bits and all) or don't go.
- Be cautious—everything is on the record.
- Be organized—choose a designated speaker, with colleagues to fill in blanks where necessary.
- Be interesting—bring someone Board members will want to meet, make sure your presentation is topical, and stick to what you know.

News Conferences

WHEN TO HOLD A NEWS CONFERENCE: ALMOST NEVER

Given the risks and expense of holding a news conference in an empty room, this publicity technique should be reserved for the rarest occasions. In fact, news conferences are much more useful in managing the media when you have too much news than they are in attracting publicity when you haven't had enough. If you have a compelling speaker, an interesting and important story that benefits from explanation, stunning visual aids, or if you have too many reporters knocking on your door, think about calling a news conference. Otherwise, send a news release.

WHEN TO HOLD A NEWS CONFERENCE: WHEN THE ALTERNATIVE IS WORSE

While generally to be avoided, a news conference can be the perfect solution when you are trying to manage media attention during a crisis or other fast-breaking news story. Media calls can overwhelm your executive team—and reporters can get angry if they think the competition has better access. It's best to make yourself available to everyone, at regular intervals, answer all the questions you can, and then decline further inquiries pending the next conference. Reporters then know when to get you—and know they won't get scooped.

TREAT EVERYONE FAIRLY, BUT DON'T TREAT THEM THE SAME

Having gathered a large group of reporters together, don't make the mistake of treating them all the same. Different media have different needs.

- TV cameras need a view, and a good picture.
- Print reporters need detail.
- "Local" reporters want a "local" angle.
- Reporters from the ethnic media might need translation.

Attend to these details, and book enough time to answer questions thoroughly. Also, watch for those reporters whose audiences might have a particular interest in your issue. You shouldn't show favoritism, but you should try to ensure that everyone gets the answers they need.

CASE THE JOINT: MAKE SURE YOU HAVE THE RIGHT VENUE

As with any meeting, be careful to book your news conference in the right room. Jamming lights, cameras, and action into too small a space makes people irritable, while hosting three reporters in a cavernous ballroom will suggest that your event is already a disappointment. Think about heat, light, power, and the public address system. (Don't rely on media for microphones or tape.) Think about access (and parking) for the media and about egress for yourself. That is, make sure you have a clear exit; you never know when you might need it.

Setting the Agenda: Take Control

Whenever you assemble a crowd of reporters, you should be clear about your purpose. The lead-off speaker at every news conference should set an agenda, spell out the ground rules, and, especially in large conferences, be prepared to enforce those rules. For example, if you say that reporters can only ask one question, keep a hand on the microphone (or have the ability to turn it off). If things get out of hand or go on too long, have someone available to end the conference, hurrying the principal to "an important, previous engagement."

Setting the Agenda: Give Up Control

The best-laid plans notwithstanding, the rules still change when the cameras start running. You can tell reporters at a climate change conference that Al Gore won't talk politics, but you can't stop them from asking the question (we've tried). You can tell reporters that a news conference ends at 10:45 a.m., but you can't interrupt a long answer from His Holiness the Dalai Lama (we didn't try). News conferences are, by nature, risky. If the risk is too great, don't go there. If the risk is acceptable, be bold, be gracious, and go with the flow.

12

Building a Good Media Relationship: Living with the Grizzly

Perhaps the grizzly analogy is too strong. It might be better to think about the media like fireworks—fabulous, even beautiful, in the right circumstances, but disastrous if someone drops a match at the wrong time. Think of these as rules for sensible care and handling.

Do Your Homework

A "bad" interview can have dire consequences for any company. Executives who are unprepared for the bright lights and harsh questions of the daily news media often end up watching their worst nightmare unfold on the six o'clock news. To survive the experience, imagine a worst-case scenario. Then spend time preparing your statement or message, anticipating questions and thinking through your answers.

In TV and Radio: Build Bridges

Skillful "bridging" is critical to any successful TV or radio interview. Bridging is not a matter of avoiding questions. Rather it describes the process by which you can address a question respectfully, and then connect back to your own key messages. It's important to realize that a reporter may use only 15 seconds of a 10-minute interview. The more effectively—and more often—you can bridge from an informative answer to a critical message, the greater the chance that your key points will be included in the report.

Speak Up: Secrecy Breeds Suspicion

When speaking to the media, "No comment" sounds like you've got something to hide. Reporters love a good mystery—so do their readers. "No comment" invites suspicion and mistrust; it suggests you are trying to hide something—even if you are not. Although legal or business considerations may limit your response, a general willingness to respond openly to media inquiries is usually the best policy.

Keep It Brief

If you talk too much during a media interview, you increase the likelihood of your statements being used out of context or your most important point being lost in the discussion. Television and radio news interviews feed on short interview statements: 10 to 15 seconds is about average. Keep your comments short and focused.

Use Plain English

Public statements made in media interviews or news releases should use everyday English. Although technical or legal advice must often be considered when preparing a statement or news release, the public message should always be clear, compelling, and jargon-free.

Set the Record Straight

If your company's spokesperson is misquoted or a news story contains serious errors, correct them. Call or write the reporter directly. Be courteous—don't blame or scold—but be firm in asking for a correction, even if that means moving on to senior editors or producers with your complaint. Also, ask that the Internet versions of the story be updated or removed. It is important to ensure the error does not pop up in future stories about your company. That said, don't expect the correction to receive the same prominence as the original story. Except in the rarest of circumstances, they never will.

The 15-Minute Rule

Few things are more annoying or puzzling to a reporter than being unable to reach a company that has just sent them a news release. So, before you send out the news release and book yourself into a day of meetings, consider: It's not a good idea to annoy someone who is about to write a story about you. Nor is it wise to have a reporter rewriting your news release when they still have unanswered questions. So, when a news release goes out, make sure the person identified as the contact will be available to take media calls. If the contact is unavailable when a reporter calls, he or she should be able to return the call within 15 to 30 minutes.

Don't Dignify Petty Criticisms

It's tempting, when you are criticized in the media, to rise vigorously in your own defense. But it's often the wrong thing to do: You may unwittingly call attention to criticism that no one noticed, and you give your critic credibility by responding. If someone says something that is damaging to your business or reputation, by all means respond. But if someone says something critical, hurtful, or even untruthful, assess the damage. If there isn't any, seriously consider letting it pass.

Media Bashing: A Short-term Pleasure

It's sometimes tempting to demonize the media, to point out their failings, and, in dramatic cases, to refuse to deal with them. This is risky. You should always move decisively to correct inaccurate media reports, and to challenge media bias if it is easily demonstrated. But surveys show that the public appreciates the media's watchdog role. And castigating all media can create hostility where there was none. It is naïve, especially in politics, to think of media members as your friends. It's worse to make them your enemies.

There Is No "Off the Record"

Always assume that anything you say when speaking with a reporter is on the record and could end up in print or on the air. If you feel compelled to go "off-the-record," do so only with a reporter you know and trust and only after you have agreed how your comments are to be used. But always remember, there is no reliable guarantee that off-the-record information won't ultimately be used.

Expect Less

While nearly all established radio, television, and print media bind themselves to an ethical code, "new media"—especially Internet blogs—are less predictable. It's partly a question of approach (new media pioneers sometimes pride themselves on being outrageous), and it's partly a question of economics ("old" media have assets and can be sued to good effect; a popular blogger may have nothing more than a short-term contract with an Internet service company). You can't ignore the newcomers; they are already too influential. Just don't make the mistake of expecting the same level of accountability.

Expect More

Companies make two common mistakes when judging media performance: They overreact to every perceived insult, or they under-react, allowing inaccuracies to stand for fear that a media outlet won't want to make a correction. Most major media abide by an ethical code that includes a responsibility to:

- Verify all information;
- Allow anyone under attack a chance to respond;
- Maintain a clear separation between editorial and advertising; and
- Correct mistakes quickly.

If you see any of these conditions breached, request redress immediately. It's your right and responsibility.

News Offers No Guarantees

Reporters are NOT in the PR business. Don't expect reporters to be an extension of your PR department. If you want your story covered, make sure it contains the elements of a news story and can withstand scrutiny. Then have a spokesperson standing by to respond to questions and provide background. If you want the messages in your news releases reproduced word for word, call the advertising department.

Be Bold, Balanced, and Brief—and Tell a Story

Here are three easy rules to help ensure that the point you want to make in a TV interview doesn't get lost in editing or dismissed by your audience as biased:

1. Speak with conviction.
2. Don't overstate your point of view. Be objective.
3. Make your point in 15 seconds or less.

It is also good to prepare brief examples and anecdotes to illustrate your point. The more complex the story, the more likely it is that a ready example or illustrative story will connect with an audience that has no expertise in your field.

Mastering the TV Interview: Dressing for Success

A television appearance needn't be an exercise in costuming, but you should know what works and what doesn't. In general, avoid checks, plaids, patterns, and mono-color combinations. Simple contrasting colors work best. For example, men can never go wrong with a light shirt, a blue blazer, and a bold, solid-color tie. If in doubt, ask the producer ahead of time what the set is like and whether others will be dressed casually or formally—and bring along some clothing options just in case. Finally, don't rely on the crew to tell you if your shirt is untucked. Look in the mirror.

Avoiding—or Recovering from—a Stupid Mistake

The halls of ignominy are crowded with intelligent and well-intentioned people who got their "mords wixed" on national television. In the face of the bright lights—or any public attention—always start by taking a breath. Pause. Ensure your thoughts are in order before you speak. If necessary, ask people to repeat a question. And when you make a public mistake, don't hide. In an embarrassing moment, nothing redeems you more than getting back on the horse. An apology and a brave smile may not undo all the damage, but it shows you have grit.

When NOT to Talk to the Media

Usually, when you get caught in controversy, your first response should be to speak up and get your story out. But there are occasions when it's necessary to hold off. When legal issues are involved, or when the details of a story are still becoming clear, you can often do damage by speculating. You may also breathe life into a controversy by offering "no comment" in response to inflammatory questions. So, speak clearly and quickly when you have news. But don't be drawn into doing interviews before you are ready.

13

Social Media: Moving From Confrontation to Conversation in an Age Redefined by the Internet

The emergence of alternative—and interactive—sources of media has forever changed the relationship that would-be communicators have with the ever-more-integrated "public." Clumsy companies will find this new "social media" curiously resistant to traditional manipulation. Smart companies will find a new and liberating opportunity for a productive conversation with their most important stakeholders.

Social Media: Ending the Age of the One-Way Message

In this past revolutionary decade, Google, Wikipedia, Facebook, and Youtube, as well as blogs and all the other e-mail groups and Internet forums, have emerged as interactive alternatives to traditional media. These "social media" have made it impossible for any business—no matter how powerful—to dominate the news with a single, one-sided message. There are too many independent sources, too many checks and balances. In that light, honesty, sincerity, and transparency—which were always positive PR elements in a public conversation—are now more critical than ever.

World Wide Web-crawling: Finding Friends in Unlikely Places

In the recent past, companies and organizations had only two chances to reach out to the public: They could court media coverage (with its attendant risks) or they could advertise (often at huge expense). Today, a simple (and relatively inexpensive) website can make your point of view available directly to people in every corner of the world––with no worries about how that information will be "interpreted" by reporters. People won't necessarily pay attention, but if something goes wrong (or something goes right) Google will bring the world to your door. Make sure you are ready.

Search Engine Marketing: Get Good Advice

It's tempting to think that a beautiful website, alone, will bring the world to your door. But searchbots need help. For example, if your mission statement is embedded in a front page graphic, search engine software won't be able to read it. So, if you want to be noticed, make sure that your website is designed and written in a way that is easily searched and indexed. Bear in mind too that this is an evolving specialty. You may have to engage an additional consultant to the one who builds your web page.

Finding an Authentic Voice: Speaking the Internet Lingo

The tone and nature of Internet conversation is quicker, more casual, and often more belligerent than in other business or media applications. So if you intervene online using a formal, corporate voice, you risk dismissal or derision. But be careful not to let the casual format lull you into carelessness. You may think you are speaking on a small blog to a bunch of kids, but you could easily hear those words quoted back to you in a boardroom—or in the *New York Times*. If you are on the Internet, you are on the record.

Honor Your Critics: They Could Become Your Best Friends

Any time you respond effectively to a customer's complaint, you have an opportunity to build real loyalty. So honor your critics online. Listen for legitimate complaints and respond with temperance and good faith. This can be a challenge because the medium is littered with "trolls," snarling vandals who take pleasure in getting people riled up for no reason. High-profile sites also attract the attention of trolls-for-hire, people who do dirty work for the competition. Avoid the muck, assume most people who comment on your site are legitimate and you will find friends in the mix.

Keep an Ear to the Ground: Internet Drums Can Be Silent When Deadly

Every major corporation monitors mainstream media, but it's tougher to keep track of the Internet. With millions of blogs addressing millions of issues, you never know when you might become the object of someone's attention. Try to keep track. Stories originating on small blogs often find their way onto the blogs Daily Kos, Huffington Post, or the Drudge Report, reaching more people than the *Wall Street Journal*. And sometimes these stories won't make the leap to mainstream. So someone should be watching, so you can see trouble coming and correct misinformation.

Reasons to Avoid Social Media: It's a Black Hole Where Time Disappears

The Internet is brimming with opportunity—it's full of applications that you might use to expand your customer base or your social network. But if some 25-year-old consultant tells you that you should sign up for Facebook, Friendfeed, Flickr, Twitter, LinkedIn, and MySpace, ask why. Each of these applications can consume large parts of your day—in little, hardly noticeable increments. Make sure that every online effort has a sensible and attainable strategic goal.

Reasons to Avoid Social Media: You Don't Want to Be Dissed as a Tourist

Six weeks before the last election, Canadian Prime Minister Stephen Harper had a website hot-buttoned to every new social media application available. But the PM himself was nowhere to be seen. There were no comments on Twitter. The "About Me" section was blank on MySpace and he had only six friends. His YouTube account linked to four, six-month-old videos. The result? What seemed like an effort to make it LOOK like the Prime Minister is hip to the Internet, demonstrated instead that he is NOT.

14

Communicating in Crisis: Keeping Your Head, and Your Reputation

There is a sense among certain Asian cultures that a crisis is actually a gift—it is an opportunity to show your mettle, perhaps to demonstrate both courage and humility. Be that as it may, a crisis certainly presents a moment in which you can watch things get worse or start to make them better. Here are some steps on the latter path.

Do the Right Thing

How you handle a public relations crisis can do more damage to your reputation than the crisis itself. (Think about Richard Nixon's worst days in Washington, D.C. and Rudy Giuliani's best days in New York City.) Crisis management is a character test. Business people who prevent a crisis from becoming a nightmare have a common approach. (Here comes that big tip once more:)

1. They do the right thing.
2. They are seen to be doing the right thing.
3. They don't get #1 and #2 mixed up.

That is, they don't treat the crisis simply as a PR problem. Nor do they assume people will automatically understand or believe that they have done the right thing.

Transparency 101: Rip the Band-aid Off Quickly

In the face of a public relations crisis, one common (and very human) response is to huddle behind closed doors, circle the wagons, and hope it all blows over. Resist this urge. It invites the wrath of reporters and it alienates the public. Although there are exceptions, getting your whole story out, as quickly as possible, is usually the fastest way to get off the front page.

Transparency 201: Covering the Basics

In addition to sticky details that might damage your reputation, in a crisis, reporters and the public want the basics—the who, what, where, when, why, and sometimes how. Gather this information quickly so you can answer three basic news questions:

- What happened?
- What are you doing about it?
- How will you make sure it doesn't happen again?

Report what you know. If you don't know something, don't speculate. Admit you don't know, say that you'll try to find out, and tell them when you'll report back. Reporters will get answers; it's best if they get them from you.

Transparency 301: Managing Other Sources

It's never a good idea to try to *manage* the news, especially during a crisis. But if it's *your* crisis, you have to take responsibility for the accuracy of information being reported in the media—no matter the original source. There is no perfect way to do this, and no way to prevent damaging and erroneous rumors completely, but you should monitor all news outlets, assess the public's reaction to stories, and *correct damaging errors immediately*. Be quick to apologize for misinformation even if you are not the source. It will demonstrate your reliability, responsibility, and concern.

Don't Take the Bait

In the worst part of a crisis, it's always wise to expect criticism, no matter how well you are handling the actual issue. Criticism from the media or the public, or from your customers, employees, or other stakeholders may be unfair—and it will often seem excessive, especially when you are doing everything you can to deal with an issue. But a sharp rejoinder will just heat things up. Take the high road. Acknowledge people's concerns, but avoid being defensive or overly apologetic. Stay calm and explain what you are doing to deal with the problem.

Perception as Reality

In crisis, there is often a gap between public perception and operational reality. But if the public thinks you have a crisis, you have a crisis—no matter what your engineers say. And the larger the gap between what you know and what the public believes, the bigger the threat to your credibility. Here is what you must do:

- Identify why communication gaps exist (normal media skepticism, industry reputation, rumors).
- Distribute information that addresses those gaps.
- Recruit credible experts to confirm your facts.

Close the gap or the reputational crisis will long outlast the operational crisis.

Before You Speak, Listen

An audience that is angry or fearful won't listen to you if they don't believe you're listening to them; you must understand the audience's feelings, knowledge, and preconceptions. So do your research. Hold meetings. Conduct focus groups. Launch telephone surveys. This will inform your strategy by eliminating guesswork, establishing what your audience knows and what they need to know, measuring the effectiveness of your communications and the relevance of your messages. It can also guide your response (if no one other than you thinks it's a crisis, you may not want to draw greater attention by speaking out).

Recognize Crisis as a Test of Character

The intense scrutiny that comes in a crisis carries a huge risk—and a potential reward. People are watching for two things: the competence you demonstrate in dealing with the crisis; and the concern that you show for your employees, for public safety, and for the environment. Put your own financial interests to the fore and people will punish you long after the crisis abates. But if you concentrate on doing the right thing—regardless of the short-term damage to your bottom line—you may come away with a reputation that's actually better than it was going in.

Ensure Adequate Communication Capacity

In most crises, there will be information that is important to shareholders, customers, clients, employees, and their families—but of little interest to the media. You must have a means of communication capable of handling large volumes of inquiries: set up a toll-free number, add extra phone staff, and most effective, set up a website with all the answers and a way of sending you queries. If you already have one, you should create a backup—a "dark site" that is ready for launch in an emergency.

Manage Media Expectations

You will be shocked in crisis by how many reporters there are and by how much time they can absorb in separate, unscheduled, but urgent interviews. If you try to ignore this onslaught, you will find reporters lurking everywhere—pressing employees and even family members for information. If you respond ad hoc, your management team will be so busy dealing with media, they won't be available to solve the crisis. So, set a regular time for media briefings, enabling reporters to confidently pursue other work in the meantime. Then, be sure you offer something substantive—make the wait worthwhile.

Choose Your Spokesperson Well

A well-informed, credible, and sincere spokesperson can be a blessing in any crisis. But a spokesperson who is evasive, defensive, and combative—one who takes tough questions personally—will arouse suspicion and, potentially, fear. So, choose carefully. Identify a natural communicator who is trainable—and then train them. Choose someone who is quick to grasp technical issues, but plainspoken. And choose an employee, not an outside consultant who may be seen as a "spinner." The spokesperson doesn't need to be from the executive suites, but he or she needs corporate support and authority to answer reasonable questions or explain, quickly and politely, why not.

Breaking out the Big Gun

When, in a crisis, should you put your CEO in front of the cameras? It's a tough question, with no standard answer. But here are a few considerations:

1. Would the CEO's appearance escalate the matter, making it look worse than the public had assumed?
2. Would the CEO's absence suggest a failure to stand accountable?
3. Could you arrange an appearance without risk of an embarrassing public scene?
4. Is your CEO empathetic or apt to appear brittle and unconcerned?

Cover these bases, but when in doubt, err on the side of using the CEO.

Cutting the Legs off a Story

Have you noticed those critical stories that never seem to go anywhere, but never seem to go away? It's necessary, when something big goes wrong, to make a gesture that is sufficient to prove you have taken the issue seriously. You might have to make a sacrifice, such as firing a senior member of your team. But every story has a beginning and a middle; to make it go away, you have to provide a credible end.

Good PR Means Doing Better Next Time

Last year, the Canadian postal service evacuated three floors of its Vancouver, B.C. facility because of a bomb threat, but kept employees working on the fourth floor. When some of those workers noticed colleagues clustered outdoors, they started to panic; but when they tried to leave, supervisors ordered them to stay put or suffer disciplinary measures. Canada Post says it "followed all the protocols" and that employees were not in danger. But why defend a protocol that forced supervisors to threaten ill-informed and fearful employees? It's not an admission of failure to say you'll try harder next time. And apologies are free.

Apologizing: Go Quick, Go Solo

When former *Seinfeld* star Michael Richards launched his racist tirade in an L.A. comedy club, he took three fatal swipes at his own career. First, he used the n-word; second, he took too long to apologize; and third, he let publicist Howard Rubenstein become part of the story. In an age of instant access (to inflammatory video, in this instance), you can no longer wait 24 hours to issue a "timely" apology. And if you hire a PR firm to help cover a mistake, find one modest enough to stay out of sight. Their presence signifies that you are more worried about your reputation than your wrongdoing.

Actions Trump Spin; Spin Can't Trump Action

Complaining that al-Qaida is "out-communicating America," former

U.S. Defense Secretary Donald Rumsfeld once announced a new PR push in the war on terror—including a new 24-hour media operations center and more media training for military personnel. Reacting to this news, the *Economist* magazine wrote that "winning hearts and minds is [not] just a question of better presentation . . . no amount of spin will make locking people up indefinitely without trial at Guantanamo Bay look compatible with American principles of justice." It's a PR lesson for everyone: No amount of PR trickery will save you if you are doing the wrong thing.

PR à la Cheney

When former Vice President Dick Cheney shot his friend and hunting partner Harry Whittington in the face in 2006, Cheney tried to keep the story quiet and he hid from the media. It was a case study in what NOT to do:

- First, if you don't tell your story, someone else will, and it may not be good.
- Second, if you have treated reporters with disdain, you can expect the same when you get into trouble.
- Third, a public figure caught in a cover-up is penalized twice: once for the offence and once for trying to avoid the consequences.

Panic Is a PR Faux Pas

When the International Cycling Union announced that 2007 Tour de France winner Floyd Landis tested positive for testosterone, Landis launched a scattergun defense: The tests were wrong; the results were fixed; his massage oil was spiked. . . . But experts dismissed these explanations, destroying Landis' credibility with media and fans. Later, Landis retreated to a simpler message—saying that he was innocent, baffled by the test results, and confident he'd be vindicated. Too late. In a crisis, don't get caught thinking out loud. When reporters are testing your every word, silence can be golden.

90 Percent Can Be a Failing Grade

Following the recall of 18 million lead-tainted Chinese-made toys, China's Ambassador to Canada, Lu Shumin, said that "more than 90 percent" of his country's exports are safe, adding, "This kind of problem exists everywhere in the world. So why just pick out China for a big fuss?" When dealing with a PR crisis, you make matters worse by trying to minimize the problem, by denying responsibility, or by casting aspersions at others. People want to know that you recognize the problem and that you are committed to protecting their interests, not your reputation.

Handling Bad News

Handling Bad News: Tell it Like it Is

Trying to cover up bad news with an unrealistically positive press release may please the boss, but it won't impress an experienced reporter. Successful public relations require candid discussion of both good news and bad. Corporations that "tell it like it is" develop credibility with customers, shareholders, media, and the general public. Corporations that try to get cute often create a question mark that never goes away. Deciding how much truth to tell can be tricky; but even when circumstances prevent you from telling "the whole truth," be sure you tell "nothing but the truth," confident that good solutions can follow bad news.

Handling Bad News: Respect the Public's Opinion

A company's openness and respect for public concerns will generally be reflected in more positive news coverage and greater public support. Successful public relations programs are based on genuine empathy for and understanding of public concerns. Corporations that do not acknowledge the public's right to participate in business decisions that directly affect their lives will see their reputations suffer.

15

Crisis Planning:
Preventing What is Preventable;
Preparing for Everything Else

It is in the nature of crises that not all are preventable—the best-laid plans sometimes go wrong. But that's no excuse for neglect. Crisis planning can keep you out of a heap of trouble—and reduce the damage when something actually goes wrong. Here's where to start.

Elements of a Sound Plan

A crisis communications plan must be short, up-to-date, and actionable. Policies and procedures should be readily available, but the plan itself must be practical.

Two major elements are:

1. The Crisis Response Team, complete with job descriptions for each role; and
2. A list of resources and audiences, including current contact numbers for every group or audience you might have to reach in a hurry: regulators, suppliers, employees, customers, media, advocacy groups.

You also need a crisis hierarchy chart setting out appropriate response levels to crises of increasing severity.

Strike a Planning Team

Step one in crisis communications planning is assembling a planning team, including leaders from every company department. This team must identify potential crises and response strategies. The team should also agree on principles underpinning the plan. On the day of the crisis, you don't want your spokesperson and your lawyers debating how open to be with the media. You need to have thought out the scenarios and agreed beforehand. Remember: How you respond will affect how the media responds to you. You set the tone for coverage in those first intense hours.

Assembling the Team

A Crisis Response Team should include:

1. An executive decision maker
2. Well-trained media spokespeople
3. A chairperson
4. Advisors, including technical and operational staff to provide accurate, up-to-the-minute information on the crisis and its remediation; public relations counsel experienced in crisis management, and, depending on the crisis, a lawyer.

This team should be trained and, in a perfect world, always available. Unfortunately, crises often occur when people are unavailable, so all key team members should have a solid and well-trained back-up person.

Think the Unthinkable

The second step in crisis communications planning is getting your planning team to define what constitutes a crisis for your company.

1. List all possible incidents that could damage your business or reputation—e.g., a food poisoning, an employee accident, rumors of insolvency.

2. Rank the probability of each incident.

3. Rank the seriousness (potential damage) of high probability incidents.

4. Tailor your planning, training, and prevention accordingly, focusing on potential crises that are most serious and most likely to occur, but including incidents that, although unlikely, would be devastating.

Assess Your Reputation

The reputation your company brings into a crisis will determine how well you survive it publicly. Consider doing a reputation audit. This will tell you how healthy your reputation is with your customers, employees, investors, and suppliers. Would they be supportive and give you the benefit of the doubt in a crisis? How is your company's relationship with the media? It's likely that, in addition to pointing out potential weaknesses in crisis, such an audit will also provide important information for day-to-day marketing and public relations management.

Hold Up the Mirror

Crises tend to amplify strengths and weaknesses in your management culture, so take a hard look in the mirror. Does your team bring issues to your attention or have a "don't tell the boss" mentality? Is public relations part of the executive team or simply spinning out promotional materials? Even the rigidity of your corporate hierarchy can be an issue: A top-down management style is bad news if your CEO is in Bali when the crisis hits. Take this opportunity to reduce risk by addressing management weaknesses.

Test the Plan

Once you have identified your risks, assembled a team, assessed your reputation and corporate culture, and developed a crisis communications plan, it's important to test the plan and the team. Set up a mock crisis and challenge your team to deal with it in real time.

Imagine a fire: Can you quickly access employee information if you need to contact family members? Imagine a front-page story announces your CFO is suspected of insider-trading: How would your company react? A real-time test is essential to develop your team's skills and to identify weaknesses in the plan.

16

Investor Communications: Sharing with Your Shareholders

For those in publicly traded companies, investors comprise such an important audience that it is worth considering them in their own right. Like the media, you should treat them with caution. Like employees, you should treat them with respect. Grab the kid gloves and consider some specifics.

Truth and Competence Rule

Investor relations is a marketing exercise that uses public relations to communicate with investors. Contrary to popular opinion, it's not about selling a stock. Investor relations is really about building confidence in management, which, in turn, depends on demonstrating management competence and integrity. Investors will forgive a normally competent CEO when the company fails to achieve one or two important milestones if the problems are disclosed and solved. However, investors will lose faith in a CEO who tells a lie or attempts to hide a problem.

Always Start with Research

You wouldn't formulate a marketing plan without researching the consumer appetites; likewise, you shouldn't formulate an investor relations plan before assessing the investment community's knowledge and its impressions of your company. Such an assessment, called an investor perception audit, is also a useful benchmark against which you can later measure how well your messages are getting through.

Close the Information Gap

It is not unusual for the share price of a publicly traded company to lag behind other companies in the same sector with similar performance and prospects. Often the reason is a communication gap between the under-performing company and the investment community. A company in this situation needs to understand the gap and implement strategies to close it. This should begin by asking two questions:

1. Do investors understand us?
2. Do we understand what investors expect of us?

The answers will form the basis of a more effective communications program.

Don't Blame the Media for Bad Management

Executives wondering if their company's communications with investors needs improvement should ask the following: If investors understood what is really going on in our company, would our stock price a) be higher or b) be lower? If the answer is a) higher—better investor communications are needed. If the answer is b) lower—better management is needed.

Share Your Plans; Update Your Progress

A company needs to lay out a simple roadmap for investors explaining where it is coming from, where it is going, and how it is going to get there. Then it is critical that the company regularly measure its progress against these objectives and communicate that progress—or otherwise— to investors. If this is done thoughtfully, all investors, from the least to the most sophisticated, can understand even the most complex of companies and business sectors.

Use Plain English

Publicly traded companies need to be able to describe their investment merits in plain English. Retail investors often don't have the knowledge and professional institutional investors often don't have the time to wade through long, jargon-laden prose. Sell-side analysts, who do need heaps of details to do their work, also appreciate plain English because it demonstrates the company understands how to appeal to investors. Companies that can't explain themselves concisely in plain language 1) haven't tried hard enough, or 2) don't really understand what appeals to investors.

Some Secrets Are Best Shared Quickly

It's hard to find the right balance between transparency and confidentiality, but take this as a rule of thumb: If you get asked a question from multiple investors or you spend more than 15 minutes discussing an issue, the information is probably material or at least worth mentioning in your regular communications.

Bad News Starts to Stink When It Gets Buried

There are two kinds of news releases from publicly traded companies: candid releases about successes and failures, and baloney sandwiches with bad news hidden between thick layers of promises and excuses. Keep in mind baloney detectors are standard issue for most financial journalists and investors. Publicly traded companies that try to bury bad news deep within the layers of their press releases risk more than their credibility. These days, shareholders may even sue the company for misleading them.

Loose Lips Sink Credibility

Selectivity is a good thing when choosing spouses, wine, and swimsuits. Selectivity is not a good thing when publicly traded companies curry favor by giving extra information to favorite research analysts or financial reporters. In fact, companies that selectively disclose material information violate securities regulations. Even if they evade the wrath of the regulators, the credibility of loose-lipped management will die the death of a thousand cuts from out-of-the-loop analysts and reporters.

Manage Your Stock for Value, Not for Profit

Don't focus your investor relations on managing the share price; you may find ways to inflate your stock, but the result will likely be short-lived and the impact on your credibility may be harsh and enduring. Focus on communicating a sound business plan; you will build trust and confidence, and your share price will find an appropriate and sustainable value.

Little Lies Create Big Problems

We are seeing more and more stories about senior executives who have exaggerated their education and experience in their resumes. This is a major PR crisis. Any board of directors that doesn't quickly dispatch a lying CEO is risking poisoning the company's employee pool, chasing away customers, and destroying its equity capital base. Once the offender is gone, the company's stakeholders need to see that the board has replaced its ethics committee with directors who take the job more seriously.

Mergers and Acquisitions

Your Company Is Always in Play

A publicly traded company is, by definition, always for sale. Long before an uninvited buyer comes knocking, the board and management should nurture positive relationships with all the audiences that may influence whether—and at what price—shareholders decide to sell the company. This will include business reporters who will chronicle the events for their readers, including the company's shareholders. If business reporters understand the company's achievements and know and trust its management before the first shots of a takeover battle are fired, this will be reflected in their coverage of the war that follows.

DEFEND VALUE, NOT TURF

When someone makes an unsolicited offer to acquire a publicly traded company, the company usually complains that the price is too low. Depending on the timing and the strength of its case, this can look like directors and management are defending their jobs, rather than shareholder interests. So, wherever possible, get your shareholder value messages out first. Even as the takeover target, you want to set the market's price expectation. Also, be ready to back up that value argument. And make it clear that, if it's truly in the shareholders' interests, the company is ready to support a deal.

THINK ABOUT MEDIA WHEN SETTING YOUR STRATEGY

Given the critical nature of communication during a merger or acquisition, your strategy should include a plan for getting your messages to, and through, the news media. Before the M&A storm begins, try to prepare for all the scenarios that might unfold. Ensure that directors, managers, and advisors (legal, financial, and communications) are on your side. Your media plan should have clear objectives and strategies for reaching key audiences. Then, when the M&A heats up, keep the plan close when drafting news releases or conducting media interviews. Nothing destroys credibility more than a management that is confused, tentative, and inconsistent under fire.

KEEP COMMUNICATIONS IN MIND

In the midst of a complex acquisition, when the lawyers are scrutinizing every word in every announcement, it's easy to forget that communicating clearly with all your audiences is critical to the best outcome. At such times, keep your communications staff close—on the working group daily calls and in all-important meetings. Good legal advice will ensure that agreements are sound and withstand scrutiny.

Good communication advice will ensure that you say what you need to say to all audiences (employees, investors, other bidders) along the way.

Employees Need to Hear It from The Boss

A merger or acquisition will have a major impact on the work environment of your employees, whether you are the acquirer or acquired. As CEO you owe it to your employees to tell them directly, frankly, and frequently about the M&A progress and the result you expect. This openness and honesty pays a dividend: Employees are key communication links with customers, suppliers, and the general public— and employees' attitudes and comments will help determine how your company's messages are received by these stakeholders. Better to have these links tended by informed supporters than uninformed detractors.

Strange Times May Call for New Spokespeople

During a merger or acquisition, when trading regulations restrict what you can say, it's essential that you present a credible and competent face to the media and the market. Your ideal media spokesperson should be the company's lead strategist or a key contributor; reporters want to talk to "players," not observers. Additional comment can also come from someone else who is committed to the interest of shareholders; for example, a director with a large personal shareholding or one who can demonstrate support from large shareholders. Whoever speaks on behalf of the company must be articulate and able to frame key messages in a compelling and concise way.

Keep Calm in the Storm

During hectic merger or acquisition negotiations—friendly or unfriendly—and during the tense integration period that follows a merger or takeover, companies often neglect their day-to-day business, leaving employees paralyzed with uncertainty and customers feeling neglected. Therefore, during any M&A activity, management must demonstrate to all stakeholders that: 1) you are not distracted from basic business; and 2) the merger or takeover will benefit business in the long run. The more you maintain business as usual during the M&A process, the easier it will be for employees and customers to accept any changes that may occur.

BE CAREFUL WHAT YOU PROMISE

Management of public companies contemplating a merger or acquisition must promote deals carefully. In enlisting shareholder support, you must be persuasive while avoiding the risks of overselling. First, you can't appear desperate or suggest that you need a deal; it puts your stock at risk if negotiations fall through. Second, as an acquirer, you don't want to inflate the price or encourage competitive bidders. Third, you want to avoid unreasonable expectations upon completion of the deal. Remember, in the bazaar or the boardroom, you get the best bargains when you are prepared to walk away.

YOUR SHAREHOLDERS MONITOR THE MEDIA; YOU SHOULD, TOO

In a controversial merger or a hostile acquisition, it's tempting to look past the media—to listen directly, and only, to the final arbiters: your shareholders. But shareholders read and listen to the media: you should know what they're hearing—what the other side is saying and how the analysts are reacting. So, find a reputable firm to collect all print and electronic media reports and distribute them, daily, to your working group. Then, if you start losing the media contest, you'll know to revisit your messages, tactics and/or the performance of your key spokesperson.

WE'RE ALWAYS OPEN

Around-the-clock M&A negotiations can move very quickly through bids, counter-bids, and defensive maneuvers. Communicating on a timely basis is critical to achieving a successful outcome—especially if the strategy is to get your message out first after significant events.

This will require key communications advisors to be available to management around the clock, even if that means working in shifts. You want to ensure your communicator is in good form when the time comes to turn a complex legal brief into an intelligible news release, quickly and, potentially, in the dead of night.

17

Environmental Communications: Building Healthy Relationships in a Sustainable World

No one, in this day and age, can overlook the environmental imperatives that dominate our lives. Issues like global warming have forced us all to understand that our actions have consequences. Businesses that grasp that message and assume a leadership role will limit their risks, and, ultimately, maximize their profits.

It's Better to Work It Out than Duke It Out

In the world of public opinion, what is said is often not as important as who is saying it. And when it comes to the environment, research shows that Americans trust scientists, experts, and environmental groups and have very little confidence in industry and government. Given this credibility deficit, business is not likely to win a battle for public opinion. So when it comes to the environment, it is better to look for a quiet solution than to initiate a big public debate.

Doing What's Right Is also Right for the Bottom Line

In these days of questionable corporate ethics, if you want your company to be well-positioned, consider taking a position. Ray Anderson, the CEO of Interface Inc., showed the way when he decided to turn the world's largest commercial carpet manufacturer into a sustainable corporation by 2020. Anderson has shown that environmental responsibility makes good business sense. Over nine years, Interface has saved $231 million in energy and waste disposal costs and reduced its waste output by more than 40 percent. It also reduced greenhouse gas emissions by 31 percent. And its public reputation—and share price—have drifted steadily upward. Interface was also featured as a shining example of corporate social responsibility in the popular movie, *The Corporation*.

It's Easy to Get Pushed Off the Environmental Bandwagon

Environmental consciousness is certainly part of a good brand, but it can be risky to build a corporate image with self-laudatory green ads. Some companies can justify advertising about good environmental performance, but boasting about your performance can make you a target for doubters, intent upon finding any environmental problem. It's also dangerous to look for accolades when your environmental performance is perceived as meeting a minimum acceptable standard. By all means, keep a record of your good performance, but temper the hyperbole.

Sustainability: What Does It Mean?

"Sustainability" means different things to different people. To an environmentalist, it might mean that you stop cutting down trees. To a forester, it might describe how fast you can continue to cut. This confusion has led to increased mistrust—to the point that the word "sustainability" itself may prompt a negative public reaction. So, any time you want to claim that your organization is "sustainable," make sure that you give a definition, and a way that people can weigh the truth of what you say.

Sustainability: Communicate through Action

We know the clichés: "Actions speak louder than words." "Effective communication is 80 percent performance, 20 percent telling people about it." Action, rather than words, is especially important when communicating on a subject like sustainability. Studies show that people are confused about the meaning of the word sustainability and skeptical to the point of mistrust about government and corporate sincerity. So, when it comes to sustainability, don't tell people that your organization is committed to sustainability. Tell them what you are doing to make it sustainable.

Use the Language of Accountability

In a climate of mistrust, generalities are more likely to alienate than reassure your audience. If you're talking about something that people cannot measure or confirm, you're probably saying something that they won't believe. This is particularly the case for companies trying to communicate messages about sustainability. To be credible, claims must be specific and measurable. Generalities will only expose you to charges of hypocrisy, especially if it can be argued that another part of your operation is not currently run on a sustainable basis.

Use a Human Voice

It's tempting when talking about issues that are technical or expert-driven to slip into the jargon of those experts. Don't. The public—ever more accustomed to the casual tone of the Internet—has grown skeptical of corporate speak and impatient with explanations more likely to baffle than inform. So, avoid theoretical discussions and technical language. Don't talk about "economic indicators;" talk about "jobs." Don't talk about "the environment;" talk about fresh air and clean water. If you want your issue to matter, you must speak to people about the things that matter to them.

Choose Hope, Not Hype

Good leaders inspire hope, not panic. If you try to motivate your audience by fear or by threat, that audience will turn off. This applies in all business settings, but it's especially applicable when urging action on the environment. Bleak future scenarios engender paralysis. It's also bad strategy to shame people—to embarrass them with their own contradictions. If you point out that what people do doesn't align with what they say, they are more likely to change their attitude than their actions. People want and need encouragement.

Offer Solutions

People are convinced of the value of sustainability, but they are not sure what they can do personally. They feel overwhelmed by the challenges we face, and fear that they are acting alone. But people want to be part of the solution, so give them options, point out benefits, and celebrate successes. Avoid vague policy issues like "sound land-use planning;" instead, tell people how to save money, time, and energy. Avoid the language of sacrifice ("give up your car") in favor of listing likely benefits (less traffic congestion, fewer diseases like asthma, and lower costs). People are more likely to act when they feel hopeful they can make a difference.

Let People Know They Are Not Alone

Surveys show that most Americans say that they and their friends care about sustainability—but that other people don't. This sense of isolation discourages action. Research shows that people are more likely to change their behavior if they think they are working in a community of like-minded individuals—if they think "that's what people like us do." So don't scold. Don't say, "Stop walking on the grass" (like everyone else). Say, "Thanks for joining us on the path." We get the best results, one way or the other, working together.

18

Public Speaking: Making the Most of Every Presentation

From the first conversation of the day—to the last—your preparation and presentation style will always have as much influence as the content of what you actually say. But speaking publicly and professionally warrants particular care and attention. These are the details you don't want to overlook.

Your Most Important Product Is Always Yourself

In the boardroom or at the podium, the way you present yourself and your message will have an overwhelming impact on your personal and professional success. Formal presentations are critically important in this regard, but they needn't be intimidating. You don't have to be a great entertainer to give good presentations. You just need a few basic skills, good preparation, and material that you find interesting yourself. The following series will cover the fundamentals. Pay attention to these basics—and add your own passion—and your presentations will surely succeed.

Know Your Audience

The first step in creating an effective presentation is assessing your audience. You need to know precisely what you hope to achieve by addressing them, and what they hope to get by listening to you. Find out how many people will be in the room; what are their backgrounds; how familiar are they with your subject matter—are they interested already or must you capture their attention? If you understand your audience and have a clearly defined intent, you increase immeasurably the chances of conceiving a presentation that is relevant and interesting.

Do Your Best by Preparing for the Worst

Nothing will puncture your speech or presentation faster than a difficult question poorly answered. That hissing sound is the air leaking from your credibility. Preparing to answer difficult questions is as important as preparing your presentation. A tough question answered directly with composure enhances credibility with your audience.

Public Speaking: The Risks and Rewards of Winging It

Most people have been impressed at some point in their lives by a speaker who could be scintillating off the cuff, who just seemed to grab one great idea after the other out of the air. So it's tempting, as a presenter, to want to emulate that style. And in rare cases it could be the right thing to do if you have easy command of the material and if the risks of an error are negligible. But if the stakes are high—and you're not completely confident—work up a prepared text. Even if you memorize it and only refer to it for prompts, the discipline may save you from making a serious mistake.

Building a Presentation

A good presentation is like a good story: It needs a beginning (a clear introduction that sets out your direction), a middle (a solid, well-organized discussion), and an end (a conclusion that draws the whole piece together). To begin, you should be able to describe, in one sentence, what you hope to achieve, and what you believe the audience will learn. Then, set out a brief outline—a list of points that will provide a roadmap to help people follow along. Work through your points, build to a conclusion, and, finally, restate your one-sentence thesis.

Case the Joint

A last critical component in preparing a great presentation is the venue check. If you can't familiarize yourself with the room ahead of time, you should go early, check the sightlines and the sound—look for any unusual challenges caused by the space—and double check any audio-visual aids. You should also ensure that your host has correct information for your introduction. Finally, once on stage, greet the audience before turning on a PowerPoint or slide projector. You are not a narrator, you are the main event; make sure the audience knows it.

Be Conversational

Whether presenting to a small or large group, you want your audience to be thinking about what you are saying—your content—not judging your presentation style. So don't lecture. Don't affect unnatural vocal mannerisms or use pretentious vocabulary. Speak just as you would if the conversation was one-on-one. That doesn't mean that you should be overly casual in appearance or language; the appropriate level of formality should come from your content. But the best way to make your listeners comfortable and receptive is to speak plainly and conversationally—just as you usually do.

Play to Your Strengths

There are presentational elements—like humor or dramatic hand gestures—that some people use to good effect. But regardless of how they work for others, if they don't come naturally, they won't work for you. If you generally talk with your hands, don't stop. If you usually make jokes, keep it up (assuming the content is appropriate). You also want to concentrate on material that you are passionate about, and avoid invitations to present on material that you don't find interesting.

You make your audience comfortable by being comfortable—in the way you express yourself as well as in what you express.

Be Brief and Well-Rehearsed

Everyone appreciates brevity; no one ever complains if you take less time than you are given. Audiences also like a bit of polish—the clarity and familiarity you can only achieve if you are well prepared. Practice. Run through your presentation alone and, then again, with someone whose feedback you trust. See if you can make your points in less time. Some people find it helps to write out their whole presentation, even if they ultimately use a bullet-point reminder sheet. A prepared text helps you organize your thoughts and will prevent you rambling on unnecessarily.

The Power of the Pause

There are few things that will improve your public speaking as much as learning to pause, to breathe, to collect your thoughts. A pause is not "dead air;" it only seems so when filled with a panicky "um." Rather, five or 10 seconds of silence can add emphasis. It can give you a chance to think about your next point, and give your audience a chance to digest your last. The pause is especially useful when answering a question: Honor the questioner with a thoughtful response and you will be appreciated for having done so.

Look 'Em in the Eye

Whenever making presentations, look your audience members straight in the eye. Don't stare at the speech or the screen: Make eye contact and make your points directly to individuals. Your willingness to look people in the eye connects you to them. It conveys confidence and credibility. It compels your listeners to pay attention and it enables you to read the crowd, to get feedback. Then, when you pause—for breath or to think—look away; this signals a break for everyone and prevents unnaturally long and uncomfortable periods of eye contact.

Finish "Up"

One of the most common presentation errors is to finish a sentence with your nose buried in your notes, searching for the next point. If you want listeners to accept that what you are saying has value, you must deliver it with conviction—and trust that they will bear with you as you find your next paragraph or your next slide. This is especially important on a point you want to emphasize: Finish with your head up, make some eye contact, pause to let it sink in, and continue.

Fielding Questions

The best part of a presentation often comes at the end when you are answering questions. When a questioner rises, listen closely and be seen to be listening. Make eye contact. Repeat the question if it was unclear or if the audience may not have heard. Pause. Then, answer as specifically and briefly as possible, without piling on detail that wasn't requested. If you don't know the answer, say so. If the question illustrates one of your points, say so. And if it doesn't, move on: The next question may be magic.

Confrontational Questions

Any time you are faced, as a presenter, with an angry, accusatorial, or otherwise confrontational questioner, remember: Your job is to answer the question, not the attitude. Don't be defensive. Don't make excuses. Listen, calmly and patiently. Pause, to assure you are composed in response and to show that you are giving the question due consideration. Then answer as directly and dispassionately as possible. You can't necessarily make the questioner happy, but you can avoid making things worse by not raising the temperature yourself.

Beware the Techno-crutch

Technology can be a wonderful tool in the hands of a competent presenter. Illustrations, maps, drawings, thoughtful lists of critical points—all these can help give a presentation color and depth. But that doesn't necessarily mean that technology will help your presentation. Before you reach for the slides and maps or the overhead lists, think critically about their relevance to your point—and whether turning the lights down low will help you keep your audience's attention. If the technical or visual aids are relevant and informative, don't hesitate. Otherwise, avoid the distraction.

A Great Presentation Begins With a Single Step

Any would-be golfer knows the risks of trying to fix too many things at once, especially right after a lesson. The result can be just as disastrous at the podium as on the fairway. If you hope to change your presentation style for the better, pick one element at a time. Start with learning to pause and take it, slowly, from there. Audiences want only two things: good content and a shorter speech than they were expecting. Be prepared, be concise, and be confident, and your audiences will be delighted.

The Do's and Don'ts of PowerPoint

In General: Don't

PowerPoint—a brilliant innovation in presentation technology—has, in many instances, become an obstacle between a presenter and his or her audience. PowerPoint can invite carelessness, as people jot down a few points on a set of slides and then wing it. It can be distracting—with titles that fly about and land with a thud—or it can be dull, as when presenters stand and read the information on the slide. If you have graphs, maps, illustrations, or a large number of point-form lists that are essential to your topic, PowerPoint is perfect. Otherwise, park it.

If You Do: Be Brief, Be Brilliant, Be Gone

The phrase "Death by PowerPoint" was coined to describe those excruciating presentations that are all plod, no pizzazz. Consider, instead, the new Pecha Kucha format. "Pecha Kucha" is Japanese and, roughly translated, means "chit-chat." In the PowerPoint world, it describes a presentation including exactly 20 slides that stay up for 20 seconds each, using up exactly six minutes and 40 seconds. The format may not work perfectly for your own presentation, but it's a good discipline. Start here. Focus your thoughts, cull your slides, and the ultimate result will be much better.

The Winning Wardrobe

PEOPLE REALLY DO JUDGE BOOKS BY THE COVER

Wherever you present yourself in public, your appearance—your personal presentation—forms an important part of your message. Dress well and it will add to your credibility and increase your audience's comfort level. If you are too casual, too flamboyant, or in some other way inappropriately attired, it will detract from your message. So, research your audience and assess the speaking opportunity. Don't wear pinstripes and stiletto heels to pitch an organic food convention; don't wear a hemp suit to a meeting of bankers. When in doubt, dress up rather than down. People appreciate the effort.

CHOOSE A GOOD MIRROR

If you hope to be a credible presenter, make friends with a mirror. Always make sure before walking on stage that your audience will be thinking about your message, not an errant shirttail, a crooked collar, or a chunk of lunch stuck in your teeth. High-profile business people may also need a virtual mirror—a support staffer who tends to those details. Take care in choosing any such wardrobe consultant. Credibility in your field may not equate to "high fashion," so pick an advisor who understands your business goals as well as the latest style trends.

LIFE IS NOT A COSTUME PARTY

Some people look great in costume, but there is a time, a place—and a considerable risk if you might wind up with an inappropriate photo in the news. So, be careful before deciding to play dress-up, even if doing so might help you "fit in" with a particular audience. Be especially cautious around photographers who want you to dress up or pose in a funny position or with amusing props for an "interesting" feature photo. Their priority is likely different than yours and you don't want to sacrifice your credibility on the altar of fame.

19

Research: Know Your Audience and Know Yourself

Life always unfolds more smoothly when you act on what you know––not on what you *think* you know. Research is critical to good public relations, just as it is critical to the preparation and execution of all successful plans. Here's some of what you know—and directions for finding out the rest.

RACE Formula Defines Good PR

The best public relations is research based. Step one, if you hope to influence public opinion, is establishing a starting point:

1. Research the existing opinions and attitudes of your target audience.
2. Analyze that information, using it to prepare a communications plan.
3. Execute your plan; and,
4. Review your efforts and monitor your impact.

In the PR business, that process is captured in a formula called RACE: Research, Analyze, Communicate, and Evaluate. Remember that acronym and it will bring discipline to all of your public communications.

Research: Where Every Good PR Plan Starts

It's not impossible to influence public opinion in a vacuum, but it's a bad idea. Good public relations always starts with thorough research. Whether you use opinion polls, focus groups, personal interviews—or you just sit down and read every piece of available information—you should always begin by identifying the attitudes, issues, and opportunities that you currently face. This will help you to understand the public relations landscape. It will also give you a baseline against which to measure success (or failure) of any subsequent action plan.

Analysis: Closing the Gap Between Knowledge and Wisdom

In preparing an effective public relations campaign, research is the first step. The second is analysis—making sense of your focus group results, public opinion polls, background reading, etc. You start by answering these questions: Where do I want to go? What obstacles do I face, and how can I overcome them? What opportunities are available, and how can I make the most of them? This will help you understand your findings, put them into context, and, perhaps, reveal research gaps you need to fill before creating an informed, strategic, and measurable communications plan.

Communication: The "Action" Stage in Public Relations

Winning an argument, winning an audience, winning over a wary member of the media—all these demand careful, compelling communication. So, when preparing a communications strategy, choose your words wisely, and listen even more carefully than you speak. Once you have done your research—once you have defined your audience and analyzed the barriers and opportunities to spreading your message effectively—you must create a communications strategy that will resonate with that audience. Be sure to set measurable objectives so you can evaluate your success. Then listen carefully to see how audience members receive and understand your messages.

EVALUATION: CLOSING THE COMMUNICATIONS LOOP

You would never have a conversation without watching your listeners' reactions. Are they smiling? Are they frowning? Are they looking from their watch to the door? This attentiveness is equally essential in executing a public relations campaign. After you research and analyze your subject matter and launch a communications phase, you must evaluate your success. Ideally, you will have created measurable objectives that make it easy to follow up. Is your message reaching your audience? Are they responding? If not, the evaluation phase gives you an opportunity to fine-tune (or, sometimes, overhaul) your campaign for an ultimate success.

Survey Public Opinion: Treat the Result Judiciously

It is critical, in crafting a useful PR strategy, to understand public opinion, and the best way to do that is through professional public opinion surveys. But it is equally critical that you interpret survey results carefully. Depending upon what's on the front page that day, the public mood can swing wildly. And public attitudes evolve from raw opinion which can be easy to change, to considered opinion which can be extremely firm. If you hope to affect opinion, you need to understand where you are in the cycle, and how entrenched the public is in its views.

Missing the Point of Polling

Opinion polls seem seductively simple, but before you use them to make business decisions, be sure you understand what they're saying. For example, pollsters often report the top 10 issues of the day, citing surveys that inevitably rank political issues high and things like the environment low. These "top-of-mind" polls only really identify what people thought of first, not what they care about most; when subjects are asked to choose from a specific list, the results are often much different. So, when reading polls, don't just look at the answers; make sure you understand the questions.

Media Audits: Taking a Public Relations Pulse

Whenever you launch a new product, enter a new market, or just find a sudden increase in your public profile, you should begin with a thorough media audit of the companies and issues in the field. Accessing databases such as Factiva, Infomart, and Nexus, you can survey all recent media coverage, learning what people are reading and identifying opinion leaders. Then, you should establish an ongoing media monitoring function. This will keep you current on what's being said about you—and will guide your decisions when you are trying to get new publicity or to correct faulty coverage.

Google Yourself: Everybody Else Is

The world's biggest Internet search engine has changed forever the definition of "reputation." It's no longer possible to hope that a public relations crisis will "blow over" once an unfortunate story slides off the front page of the daily newspapers. Bad stories—or good—can hang around on Google's front page for years. So, check regularly to see what face you and your business are showing to the Google world. You might not be able to change what you find, but you should be ready to answer any questions that might arise because of it.

Mining the Internet for Information You Need

The Internet's endless information can be a blessing—or a curse if you let the detail overwhelm you. One way to organize your reading is by setting up RSS feeds from favorite news websites or blogs. Once selected, an RSS (which stands for Really Simple Syndicate) will stream new information to a "feed reader" on your computer, bringing all of your pre-selected searches together in one spot. In PR or company communications—whether tracking your clients' reputations or your competitors' innovations—RSS feeds can save you spending the whole day trolling the Internet.

20

Community Relations: Recruiting Friends and Influencing Critics

In issues ranging from real estate development to the siting, permitting, and construction of industrial operations that may (or may not) have an environmental impact, conflicts are often inevitable and government intervention is sometimes inescapable. But both can be minimized by careful conversation among all the interested parties—and a sincere consideration of all of their interests. People who hope to find the "tricks" in community relations will always wind up disappointed. But people who learn to consult well are much more likely to find success.

Listen to the Public BEFORE They Start to Scream

Often, before you embark on a major project that affects the community, regulators will require you to consult with the public. This doesn't have to be painful or counterproductive. On the contrary, the right consultative approach may enrich your plan and improve its likelihood of success. A well-designed community relations process is one part informing and many parts listening.

Do Your Homework

Good public consultation begins with good research: Learn about your neighbors. Learn the history and the current issues in the neighborhood, so you don't create or stumble unaware into an ongoing community battle. Spend some time identifying community leaders— people who have local support and credibility, people whom community members accept as representing their legitimate interests. Seek out individuals and organizations that can outline existing concerns, interests, or initiatives that may complement or clash with your development. To establish yourself in the community, you must first prove yourself to be informed and responsive.

Start Consultation Early

A careful round of community relations should be the first step in planning a real estate development or any other major project that affects the community. In real estate, especially, if you set out all the major details before consulting with community members, you'll leave the impression that consultation is a sham—that you have no intention of responding to community concerns. You'll also sacrifice the opportunity to make popular design changes early, when they're easy and inexpensive. It's best to get out early, present your general intentions, and, wherever possible, use community input to inform your plan.

Choose the Right Tools

When designing a community relations plan, remember that the first goal is to solicit public input, to understand community concerns, to incorporate solutions wherever possible, and to account for your decisions. Sometimes that process must occur in a big, overheated public meeting, but often other consultation tools are more appropriate. Consider opinion polls and surveys, focus groups, web forums, small group meetings, open houses, and, for educational purposes, brochures. Assess whether your "public" needs communication assistance, such as translators or materials prepared in other languages. And make sure that your own feedback channels—phones, faxes, websites—are open and monitored frequently.

Start Small

The first contact in a community relations outreach program should be as informal as possible. Aim for small-group meetings with the nearest neighbors—those whose interests will be most affected by your development or by the change that you are planning in an existing industrial facility. This is your first chance to assess community concerns and begin managing expectations. It is appropriate to set the scene, broadly, by describing your project and your general goals. Then it's time to solicit input: what are the fears, expectations, and desires that community members have? These are the issues that you will have to deal with; best to learn about them early.

Consultation Is Not a Sales Pitch

Remember, in the public consultation phase of a community relations process, that your purpose is to solicit input, not to sell your plan. Meetings and open houses are good venues in which to build good will, but don't just try to generate a mailing list of supporters. No such list will counter the weight of a concerted opposition. Your goal must be to listen—and to be seen listening. Establish a personal connection with participants. Don't argue or rebut. Ask why. Acknowledge and summarize input to ensure accuracy ("What I hear you saying is . . . "). It's tempting to spend the time identifying and recruiting allies, so remember, your purpose at this stage is to build trust.

If You Can't Fix it, Don't Ask About It

A critical step whenever dealing with the public comes in conceiving the questions that you want to ask. If you start soliciting feedback on issues that you can't—or won't—change, you are setting up your respondents for disappointment and yourself for a heap of grief. So, define the parameters carefully; and whatever questions you ultimately ask, be prepared to treat the answers seriously.

Strive to Make Your Plan the Community's Plan

The best way to craft an acceptable real estate development plan is to seek out and incorporate community input. Community members want to be heard. Some may be die-hard NIMBY types who will argue against any development. But others will work to resolve community concerns; welcome their assistance and you may turn critics into allies—people who will help set the mood in the all-important word-of-mouth campaign. You may also want to identify specific sponsors—credible spokespeople or interest groups in the neighborhood who can set the facts straight if needed.

When the Going Gets Tough: Listen

When faced with criticism, it's human nature to turn off—to immediately begin formulating a rebuttal. Resist this urge. Listen carefully to everything your critics have to say before you react. Sometimes people just need an opportunity to vent. And sometimes you will hear an "if"—something that you can do to resolve their concerns. Above all, don't tell people they are wrong, and don't recruit opponents by objectifying them or their position. That is, if you dismiss someone as a "radical environmentalist," then all self-described environmentalists will gravitate to your opponent's camp.

Use Interest-Based Conflict Resolution

If at any point in your process, you become unyielding in your position, your critics are likely to become just as determined to harden their opposition. This is no way to resolve a dispute. Always try to present your perspective and invite your critics to present theirs. Make an effort to look beyond "positions" to identify "interests." For example, sometimes people complain a building is "too tall" when their real concern is density, parking, shadows, or obstructed views. Ask for clarification. Often, you'll discover underlying issues that you can address.

Don't Dismiss Headline Hunters

It is always dangerous to dismiss or ignore a vocal opponent. Even if someone is demonstrably ill informed, badly motivated or isolated in the community—even if they come from outside the community and have no local support—they can still undermine a good process, especially if they can paint you as arrogant and unresponsive. Treat someone as if they are crazy and they will get crazier. Invite all your critics to participate in reasoned debate, and respond in good faith—and the community will judge you on that performance.

Monitor, Measure, and Report

The success of a community relations process rests on how well you collect, analyze, and accommodate feedback. Set out and track indicators that demonstrate the integrity of your process: how many people were consulted; how many remain engaged in the process? Report all input (summaries can be seen as biased) and give clear responses to requests and suggestions. Explain what you can and can't do, and say why. It's critical to be seen as a reliable source of all information—good and bad. If you only present one side, people will seek "balance" from your critics.

Give Municipal Councils a Solution, Not a Problem

Avoid forcing council to choose between your project and the community. Even if you can convince a municipal council or board of supervisors that a project is worthy, they are unlikely to give approval if opponents can argue that you have ignored their input. That said, you don't necessarily need 100-percent community buy-in before moving a development plan forward. Sometimes, it's enough just to do your best, especially if you can demonstrate that you have consulted in good faith and have made a sincere effort to resolve community concerns.

Keep the Faith

It is rare that any public process reveals an easy consensus. Often, serious conflicts persist long after a development is complete, and people who feel their interests have been damaged remain bitter and resentful. Even a successful consultation may feature scenes of passion and anger. Many people are unfamiliar with development processes and desperately afraid of speaking in public. Don't mistake their discomfort as irresolvable opposition. Remember: You are the community relations professional. Be open, supportive, responsive, and thick-skinned. People will appreciate your professionalism—and will be more reasonable—even if they retain doubts about your plan.

21

Employee Communications: Staying in Touch with Your Most Important Audience

They are your link to the public and the keepers of your success. They hold the key to improving your reputation and the power to destroy it. Communicate well with this audience and you will have taken the first, most critical step toward public relations success.

Keep Employees in the Loop

One of a company's most critical communication "targets" are its own employees. By communicating openly and honestly with your employees, you ensure that these essential stakeholders understand the corporate mission. By listening to their feedback, you make them feel they are part of the team. This level of communication is too important to be left to chance. Standardize internal communications, ensuring there is a regular cadence to it. That will help make employees feel included and secure—going a long way toward boosting morale and engendering employee support.

Employees with Real Input Give Real Effort

Ever wonder why after a fractious internal debate, some people resist a decision that didn't go their way, while others accept the outcome, and throw themselves into the implementation? Research suggests it's a reflection of whether they believed they had genuine input. It is not enough to give people a chance to express their views; they have to believe that the boss listened and understood. If a leader conveys genuine openness, is attentive and fair minded, team members will accept being overruled. If a decision seems foreordained, employee buy-in is much less likely.

Recognize Employees as Ambassadors

The CEO may be the public face of a company, but employees are its ambassadors. Ensure employees understand the company's plans and how they fit into them. Don't leave big questions unanswered. Don't try to cover up or gloss over bad news. Explain "why" as well as "how." Communicate clearly and frequently about company policy and direction. Word of mouth can influence your reputation. By keeping your internal messaging clear, you can increase the chance that the "word" emanating from your own organization is accurate and on mission.

The Messenger Should Suit the Message

When communicating important news to employees, it's important that the right person does the talking. Big-picture news is best coming from the top; but in general, employees prefer to hear news that affects them from their immediate supervisors. It's also important to release information in the right order. "Cascading" information helps avoid leaks and ruffled feathers and minimizes the opportunity for misinformation. All managers should have tool kits that define the corporate vision and objectives—and explains how their team fits in—to help them communicate effectively to the people under their direction.

Keep "Remote" Workers Close

As the number of mobile workers grows and companies become more and more reliant on telecommunications to get the job done, it's increasingly important to include your remote workers—those who work from home or in satellite offices—in your regular communications. Isolated from day-to-day office chat, remote workers are often the ones most in need of information. E-mail, intranet, and text messaging are all good communication tools, but remember that face-time is still key. Regular visits to satellite offices and frequent gatherings for consultants will help garner employee support and build a cohesive workforce.

Assess Your Communication Success

Regular audits are a great way to identify strengths and weaknesses in your organization's internal communications. Don't just do one when there is big change afoot; even when things are quiet, an audit will reveal how effectively you are reaching all your employees and how you can improve the way you communicate. Once you undertake an audit, make sure to report the results back to everyone so that they know their opinions were heard.

About the Authors

Beginning with his first press conference in 1972, **Jim Hoggan** founded and built Hoggan & Associates into one of the most successful public relations firms in Canada. Indeed, Hoggan & Associates won one of the Public Relations Society of America's highest honors, a Silver Anvil Award for Excellence in Crisis Communications for Business. Jim developed his expertise managing difficult issues for government, industry, and not-for-profit organizations in North America, Europe, and Asia. A law school graduate with a long-standing interest in social justice, Jim is also a leading authority on public perceptions about business, the environment, climate change, and sustainability. Chair of Canada's most influential environmental organization, the David Suzuki Foundation, Jim is also a trustee of the Dalai Lama Centre for Peace and Education; chair of the Canadian chapter of Al Gore's organization; The Climate Project; and co-founder of the influential climate change website DeSmogBlog.com. Jim has always been a keen student and an unflinching critic of his own, self-regulating industry—and much of the wisdom gathered in his wide-ranging career is collected in these pages.

Richard Littlemore spent 20 years as a writer and editor in some of Canada's most influential newspapers (the *Ottawa Citizen*, the *Vancouver Sun*) before striking off for a freelance career as an award-winning magazine writer, consultant, and as speechwriter for some of the country's most senior business and academic leaders. In the 1990s, he was also a director on the Metro Vancouver board. Richard is the Senior Writer and Strategist at Hoggan & Associates and the Editor-in-Chief of the award-winning DeSmogBlog. This is one of two books (with *Climate Cover-up)* that Richard has written with Jim Hoggan in the last year.